MW00453564

"On the interface between theology and counseling nebulous than forgiveness. Here, Bryan Maier provides careful analysis of what forgiveness is and isn't (for example, it's not just being nice, or mentally reframing the alleged offense, or coming to 'understand' the offender, or forcing oneself to 'feel' different), and ties the nature of forgiveness to the gospel itself. This short book not only helps us grasp what forgiveness is, but ties this understanding to the hands-on ministry of the pastor-counselor. Highly recommended."
—D. A. Carson, Research Professor of New Testament, Trinity Evangelical Divinity School

"Bryan Maier brings the double perspectives of theological acumen and counseling competence to bear on the questions of forgiveness and justice. He tackles definitional questions with great care and critical insight. He clearly knows the field of forgiveness literature. Importantly, the Scriptures richly inform the discussion, especially passages on divine and human forgiveness as well as the imprecatory psalms. No cheap grace is offered in this book, but instead a deep understanding of forgiveness, our longing for justice, and how they are to relate. Counselors and pastors alike will greatly benefit from pondering this book. I highly recommend this book and will commend it to others."
—Graham A. Cole, Dean and Vice President of Education, Trinity Evangelical Divinity School

"I was immediately intrigued when I received a draft of *Forgiveness and Justice: A Christian Approach*. Counselors have a special interest in the topic of forgiveness, especially when assisting persons who have experienced traumatizing abuse. My first thought was, I hope Bryan clarifies and illuminates a biblical-theological model of forgiveness so that I have a resource I can assign to my counseling graduate students. I think he succeeded and I am going to make his book a required reading."
—Jeffrey S. Black, Professor & Chair, Department of Counseling & Psychology, Director of Counseling Services, Oasis Center, Cairn University

"Dr. Maier makes a persuasive and entirely readable case that biblical forgiveness happens only in response to authentic repentance. You will find this book clear, logical, and pastoral in its treatment of the concepts of forgiveness, repentance, and injustice. Though forgiveness is a popular topic in mainstream literature, Dr. Maier gives a rare treat: cogent definitions and illustrations of God's view of forgiveness from Genesis to Revelation. Using case studies, the reader experiences not only a better definition of the final acts of forgiveness, but also the necessary pre-forgiveness activities of healing and repentance. Victims of injustice will find comfort and relief in knowing that the focus of the forgiveness process falls squarely on the shoulders of the offender."
—Philip G. Monroe, Thomas V. Taylor Professor of Practical Theology and Director of the Graduate School of Counseling, Biblical Seminary

"There is now voluminous literature on forgiveness, both Christian and secular, but few demonstrate the combination of theological and psychological competence found in this work. Especially notable is the recognition of the value of the imprecatory psalms for guidance in Christian life and therapy. Those working through the harm caused to them by others will be greatly helped by this book. There are other examples of the no-repentance/no-forgiveness position on human forgiveness, but this is clearly the best. One need not agree with the stance to appreciate the value of this fine example of Christian psychology scholarship."
—Eric Johnson, Lawrence and Charlotte Hoover Professor of Pastoral Care, Southern Seminary

"Dr. Maier's core insight is deceptively simple: that true forgiveness should be modeled on the kind of forgiveness God extends. When one realizes that this is neither 'unconditional' nor 'therapeutic,' the depth of what one discerns in this correlation surfaces. The author argues compellingly that genuine forgiveness values truth and values justice—a point that any victim of wrongdoing knows should matter, but all too often seems not to among those urging to just 'forgive and forget' and 'let it go.'

This book is informative, insightful, and so much more. In it, the reader will find wise solace for those who want the healing benefits of genuine forgiveness that takes seriously the damage caused by sin, the yearning for a God who really does value truth and justice, and who are not satisfied with cognitive (often self-blaming) reframings rooted in falsehood. One will walk away from this book understanding and appreciating why forgiveness and justice really are interrelated."
—R. Todd Mangum, Lester and Kay Clemens Professor of Missional Theology, Biblical Theological Seminary

"Dr. Maier has covered the topic of forgiveness with academic, theological, biblical, and hermeneutical aplomb. He strategically moves from examples to theories to definitions to what forgiveness sounds, looks, and feels like. Bryan gives his readership a peek into his counseling room, and a laugh with his family, without violating the sanctity of either. This is a must-read for deep thinkers and Christ-followers who are serious about getting forgiveness right."
—David E. Kirkner, Adjunct Faculty, Eastern University and Biblical Theological Seminary

"Christian and non-Christian counseling circles are rife with literature on the benefits and/ or necessity of forgiveness. Despite the proliferation of the topic, however, what it means to forgive is all too often assumed rather than clarified. Consequently, while people agree that forgiveness is good, there is little agreement on what it actually is. Bryan Maier's *Forgiveness and Justice: A Christian Approach* is a welcome and sorely-needed contribution that helps dispel the fog of ambiguity and misconception. He convincingly explains how the definition, conditions, and motives of forgiveness must be grounded in the gospel of Jesus Christ and confidence in the character of God, especially God's attribute of being just. One of the things I've so appreciated about Bryan over the years is his uniting of competent counseling theory and practice with substantive biblical and theological reflection. Both are apparent in in his book. If you're a pastor or professional counselor, you will find much help here, but so too will believers struggling with the pain of having been sinned against and those who long to be better able to minister to them."
—Keith Plummer, Associate Professor of Theology, Cairn University

"At long last Bryan Maier has written the salient book on forgiveness and justice. Dr. Maier's revelatory work has thoughtfully cleared the way for those seeking solace from interpersonal sin and shepherding others burdened by deficient formulations and assessments. The fastidious words on every page reveal the heart of a teacher, counselor, and pastor who is motivated to see genuine forgiveness and emancipatory justice realized and experienced by people in the fray. My heart was moved by his clear, concise, and coherent writing, appropriate critiques, and determination to empower people everywhere. *Forgiveness and Justice* is a must-read for people on the journey to healing while loving God and loving people."
—Rob Shelby, Assistant Professor of Sociology, University of Evansville

FORGIVENESS AND JUSTICE

A CHRISTIAN APPROACH

Dr. Bryan Maier

Forgiveness and Justice: A Christian Approach
© 2017 by Bryan Maier

Published by Kregel Publications, a division of Kregel, Inc., 2450 Oak Industrial Dr. NE, Grand Rapids, MI 49505-6020.

All rights reserved. No part of this book may be reproduced, stored in a retrieval system, or transmitted in any form or by any means—electronic, mechanical, photocopy, recording, or otherwise—without written permission of the publisher, except for brief quotations in printed reviews.

All Scripture quotations, unless otherwise indicated, are from the New American Standard Bible®. Copyright © 1960, 1962, 1963, 1968, 1971, 1972, 1973, 1975, 1977, 1995 by The Lockman Foundation. Used by permission. www.Lockman.org.

Scripture quotations marked NIV are from the Holy Bible, New International Version®, NIV®. Copyright © 1973, 1978, 1984, 2011 by Biblica, Inc.™ Used by permission of Zondervan. All rights reserved worldwide. www.zondervan.com.

ISBN 978-0-8254-4405-0

Printed in the United States of America

17 18 19 20 21 / 5 4 3 2 1

*To all of my students over the years
with whom I have I been privileged to
discuss and think about forgiveness.*

*I only hope that you learned as
much from me as I have from you.*

CONTENTS

PREFACE

"I would ask . . . for your understanding and for your forgiveness."

—Richard Clarke, former terrorism czar

"I am not asking you to forgive me. . . . I just want you to understand."

—The Sandman to Peter Parker in *Spiderman 3* (2007)

REASON FOR THIS BOOK

Richard Clarke, the terrorism czar during the 9/11 terrorist attacks, took the blame when he testified before the congressional committee. In his apology to the American people, Clarke asked for both understanding *and* forgiveness. For the purpose of this book, I ask the question: What exactly was he asking of the American people? I realize that Clarke was probably reading a written statement and *someone* chose those words for him. Someone decided it would be best for Clarke to ask for both forgiveness and understanding. Was he really asking for two different things or was he asking for one thing with two different names? What difference would it make if he just asked for forgiveness? Or what if he just requested that the American people merely *understand* him without asking for their forgiveness? Would he have been heard any differently? And finally, what would it look like for a nation to forgive a terrorism czar? How would Clarke know if his request had been granted?

In contrast, the Sandman clearly delineates a difference between forgiveness and understanding in his request of Spiderman. Apparently, according to the Sandman's definition of forgiveness, it is forever out of his reach, and therefore he makes it clear that he is *not* even asking for it. However, in spite of the fact that he feels ineligible for forgiveness, the Sandman has not given up hope of being understood. Thus, he shares with Peter Parker his version of how he killed Parker's uncle. This is all he wants Parker to know. After sharing, he does not seem to care if Parker responds to his request; he just turns to walk away. Why would he not wait for an answer? The question I have is, what was the Sandman hoping for? And how would he know if he received it? What makes this scene even more confusing is that the Sandman does receive an answer to his appeal, albeit unexpected. Parker does not grant the Sandman the understanding that he requested. Rather he actually says, "I forgive you." What does this mean? Does it make any difference that the Sandman asked for understanding but received forgiveness? And finally, by "forgiving" the Sandman, what did Parker actually give him?

A third example occurs way too often in our culture. A famous politician or Christian leader is exposed in a sexual sin. Immediately his or her spouse rushes to the microphone to proclaim that forgiveness is granted. Sometimes this forgiveness is granted in spite of the fact that the spouse is separating from the marriage. More often, forgiveness is granted in the context of the marriage remaining intact. But in either case, one is left wondering just what forgiveness even means in such circumstances.

If the terms "forgiveness" and "understanding" are confused in popular culture, I believe this confusion is even greater in the context of counseling. Much uncertainty remains despite the number of books written on forgiveness in the last twenty-five years. However, in all of the current work on forgiveness, the construct seems to be veering further and further away from any clear, consistent, theologically informed definition. While some recent books on forgiveness do indeed challenge the party line,[1] there is little agreement at all as to what forgiveness actually means—and the definitions that are offered do not seem to have any organic link to the Christian doctrine of forgiveness. This in turn sends an equivocal message to those struggling with issues of forgiveness in their own lives. Thus, my main reason for adding to the discussion is to further challenge these accepted views by addressing the theological inconsistencies and by providing more concrete answers to any counselor or pastor who has asked, "If I do not know exactly what forgiveness means, how can I call people that I work with to do it?"

This definitional ambiguity does not seem to bother many forgiveness writers. Criticizing one of my articles exposing this lack of theoretical clarity, one reviewer stated that researchers have just learned to live with the ambiguity surrounding the definition of forgiveness. My continued call for a more coherent (and theological) definition therefore appears out of step with contemporary research. This posture of "measure first, define later" is not new to the field of psychological research. For example, measuring the construct IQ became so exciting that actually defining what an intelligence quotient is (or even if there is such a thing) was left behind for several decades (I am aware and celebrate that this is changing). I believe something similar is happening with the construct of forgiveness. Living with conceptual ambiguity is one thing in the academic world, but when I am sitting across from someone who has suffered abuse at the hand of another, the definition of forgiveness becomes very important. This is even more acute when the person loves God and wants to please Him even in her response to interpersonal pain.*

What is the Selling Point of Forgiveness?

In spite of all of the confusion over definitions, however, the plethora of literature produced annually on the subject of forgiveness seems to agree on at least one point—that is, that forgiveness is a positive thing and ought to be done as soon as possible in response to interpersonal offense or sin. Even those who concede that forgiveness is a process still hold it up as the ultimate endpoint in response to interpersonal wrong-doing. Thus, when someone hurts me, there seem to be only two options available: immediate, or reasonably quick, forgiveness (which is always good and pretty much resolves the issue), or prolonged unforgiveness (which is always bad and leaves things unresolved). Obviously, when put this way, the choice is clear. Almost everyone would try to choose forgiveness. This absolute black and white pressure to forgive seems to be fueled from two main sources: therapeutic and theological.

In the last quarter of a century, the field of psychology has exploded

---

* For the rest of the book, I will use a hypothetical woman as a victim and a man as her offender. In doing this, I do not by any means wish to communicate that women are always and only victims and men are only capable of offending. In my counseling experience, I have counseled victims and offenders of both genders. This is merely for ease of writing and reading.

with hundreds of studies touting the incredible benefits of forgiveness. It is as if a new medication has hit the market, only this one is free and therefore available to all (although counselors who help their clients through it could possibly bill insurance companies), has no negative side effects and requires no FDA approval. This new intervention could even someday replace anti-anxiety medication and anti-depressants. Furthermore, it helps with all kinds of ailments. Not only does forgiveness help us feel better psychologically, but it can also help with physical problems such as high blood pressure, acid reflux, or ulcers (maybe even high cholesterol if I am lucky). The sky may be the limit as to what forgiveness can cure. As the list of benefits accrues, clear definitions lag behind. Clarifying what forgiveness actually means only postpones the relief forgiveness brings. The purported options are to either forgive and feel better, or try to understand forgiveness while remaining in pain.

A second source of pressure comes from the domain of theology. It is natural to think that here would be found several definitions and debates about the true nature of forgiveness and while there are some discussions in the literature about what constitutes forgiveness, the overwhelming theme of this literature is how to make forgiveness *doable*. It seems that for most the problem is not one of definition but one of motivation. Thus, the Bible is called on to provide at least two clear reasons (but not definitions) for forgiving: fear and gratitude. The first incentive to forgive is that God commands it. Refusing or stalling thus constitutes sinful behavior. This view of forgiveness primarily as a religious imperative also tends to preclude a reflective analysis of what forgiveness is or even how to do it. If God has commanded us to do something, we need to obey without question or else risk angering God, which can lead to consequences more severe than any ulcer. The second motivation is due to gratitude. The fact that we are all undeserving recipients of God's forgiveness forbids us from withholding forgiveness from those who have wounded us (so the argument goes). We assume that since it was a good thing for God to forgive us, it would likewise be a good thing for us to forgive others (again, definitional ambiguity aside). Thus, whether it is out of obligation or thanksgiving, the idea remains that forgiveness is something that must be done because "God says so."

The greater portion of most contemporary forgiveness writing tends to fall into one of these two categories. The authors appear to feel a burden to convince the reader that forgiveness is really worth doing after all. Why would they feel that they have to make this argument? Is forgiveness at its core so intrinsically *unappealing* that a case has to be made to move the human heart? Other questions also come to mind, such as: If forgiveness does not come naturally, why not? And if forgiveness is granted as a result of pressure, is it even truly forgiveness? Why is the common appeal to the benefits for the forgiver instead of the forgiven? Finally, why do many current attempts to promote forgiveness present it as a means to an end rather than an end in itself? Again, it is as if forgiveness has to be branded in such a way as to make it sell.

These are just some of my concerns with much of current forgiveness writing and why I feel that something is missing. The title for my book was sparked by the title of another book, *Forgiveness and Truth: Explorations in Contemporary Theology*, by Alistair McFadyen and Marcel Sarot."[2] The purpose of their book was to draw attention to the question of whether forgiveness, with the current set of definitions, could coexist with truth. In my book, I will ask a second and related question: Can forgiveness, according to its contemporary brands, coexist with justice?

No author writes free of bias and I am no exception. Thus I must mention one important limit and one important bias. With a topic such as forgiveness, the definition becomes even more complex when the concept involves issues surrounding both individual and corporate forgiveness. Sadly, part of the reason for the growth in forgiveness writing is the public "forgiveness" response of groups who have been victims of terrorist attacks or unfair policies. These responses vary from instantaneous unilateral forgiveness on the part of the victims to well-planned forgiveness/reconciliation ceremonies that attempt to bring victims and perpetrators together to construct something good out of these violent tragedies. As profitable as an exploration of the various methods and efficacy of corporate forgiveness would be, my book will focus almost exclusively on individuals forgiving individuals. This is partly due to space, but I also believe that individual forgiveness is the paradigm out of which any version of corporate forgiveness must emerge. Thus, while I believe the general ideas of individual forgiveness will apply to corporate forgiveness, the specific details will not be addressed in this work.

As for my bias, I write as a theologically-trained Christian counselor and I readily admit (and celebrate) that these two conditions have shaped my views. My theological background compels me to ask what God thinks of forgiveness and to what degree the Bible reveals His views. On the other hand, my work with people forces me to keep many painful stories in the forefront of my mind as I think through this very important topic. Consequently, I am not looking for a definition for definition's sake but rather to assist victimized people struggling through the ambivalence surrounding whether, how, and when they should forgive those who have hurt them. I am not naïve or arrogant enough to think that I will discover the absolute and final definition of forgiveness, but neither am I willing (nor can I afford) to give up the journey.

To individually thank all the students and friends who have sharpened my thinking on forgiveness over the years would take several pages. However, I must acknowledge the editorial help of Meredith Castor. Her contributions to the quality of this book are substantial. I would also like to thank the folks at Kregel Publications, who believed that I had something important to add to the discussion of forgiveness.

CHAPTER 1

MEASURING AND DEFINING FORGIVENESS

The concept of forgiveness carries a heavy weight—more than it can bear. It means so many things to so many people who consider it from different frames of reference—from academicians influenced by grand theological teachings to secular researchers trying to reduce abstruse concepts into manageable, bite-size units that can be studied in laboratory settings. What has evolved is a mishmash of concepts that often do nothing more than confuse and pressure those who are seeking relief from suffering. What is missing is a concrete, down-to-earth vision of forgiveness—one that is human and attainable.

—Janis Abrahms Spring

T hrough angry tears, Ellen reported that she had caught George in yet another extramarital affair—his fourth in their six-year marriage.* She had asked him to leave and would not take him back unless he agreed to counseling. George proudly justified his own behavior in light of the fact that Ellen herself had actually taken their

---

* Case studies used in this book, while disguised, are based on true cases from my counseling experience. Names are changed for privacy.

three-year-old son and moved in with an old boyfriend the year prior. After finding her and talking her into moving back in with him, George soon had his next affair to pay her back. At this point, Ellen interrupted to defend herself: "But I only moved in with Frank to get back at you for all of your affairs." George shot back with, "Having an affair is one thing, but taking my son away from me—this is going too far!" Needless to say, the session ended with a heavy feeling that we were just beginning a long and painful journey together.

A week later, it was as if I were dealing with a completely different couple. Both were smiling (although Ellen's smile was a bit more contrived) and George's posture and gait exuded confidence. When I remarked on the change, George proudly proclaimed, "We talked this week and Ellen has forgiven me for all of my affairs and now we are back living together." To my amazement, Ellen confirmed this was true. "Yes," she replied, "I have to forgive him. After all, I did have an affair, too, and I did take his son away and even though I don't go to church very often, I know God wants me to forgive." Turning to George, I asked if he had truly forgiven Ellen. He paused for a couple of seconds, as if he were deciding, and then said, "Sure, why not, as long as she promises never to do it again."

This exchange reveals several assumptions about forgiveness not unique to George and Ellen. The first and most salient assumption is the belief that forgiveness is something that can happen rather quickly, that the effects of years of cruel and demeaning behavior can be reduced as a result of one or two discussions. For Ellen and George, forgiveness is apparently a discrete act in time (not a process) that forever resolves an offense.

Another assumption of Ellen's is that personal wrongdoing on the part of the victim modifies or cancels out the sin of the perpetrator. Through her one affair, Ellen has forever forfeited her right to be upset with George for his many affairs. We might argue that four (affairs) to one hardly seems equal, but the fact remains that vows of faithfulness were broken on both sides. Perhaps George's point about Ellen taking their son away helps to even the score. The formula might be something like "one affair + taking the son = four (or more) affairs without taking the son." For George, however, the scales are still not quite balanced. Ellen still owes him somehow for the severity of her betrayal and thus he can postpone his forgiveness of her.

Finally, Ellen recognizes that God probably has something to do with forgiveness. She remembers her religious upbringing that stressed forgiveness as a response to a command of God. As painful as her life has turned out, she cannot afford to face the anger of whatever God might exist. So she tries to forgive George as best she knows how and hopes that one day he will forgive her and they can live with a little less pain.

Do George and Ellen's assumptions about forgiveness reflect anything close to what forgiveness really is? By what criteria should I, as a counselor, judge their views on forgiveness? Moreover, as a Christian, should I allow my faith to influence my professional views on forgiveness? Is there a distinctly Christian view of forgiveness or is all forgiveness the same? These questions and many more consistently emerge in my encounters with people who seek to forgive and be forgiven.

Four Conclusions of Forgiveness Literature

Contemporary research in the area of counseling and psychology points to a renewed interest in the topic of forgiveness. What was once viewed as at best a mere religious idea, and at worst a pious reinforcement for weakness, is now seen as an increasingly effective tool in helping people deal with interpersonal pain. We may draw several conclusions from this quarter-century of research that can help us in our attempt to define and understand forgiveness.

Forgiveness Is Good For You

The first and most common conclusion is that forgiveness, whatever it is, is *good* for us. Although some depict the relationship between forgiveness and health as an "unanswered question,"[1] the overwhelming conclusion of most writers in this area is that forgiveness brings at least some health benefits, including but not limited to: lower blood pressure,[2] reduced hypertension,[3] and overall better cardiovascular health.[4] Furthermore, people who are more forgiving report less stress and fewer stress-related symptoms and overall health problems.[5] One study suggests that the benefits of forgiveness could even penetrate to the cellular level,[6] while another claims that forgiveness can even reduce the severity of psoriasis.[7]

The benefits of forgiveness are not limited to the physical realm, however. Those who "take the time to go through the forgiveness process" become "psychologically healthier."[8] One of the earliest studies in this area found that forgiveness could alleviate symptoms of depression, anxiety, and even paranoia.[9] Forgiveness also builds self-esteem and eliminates the unhealthy side effects associated with holding a grudge. Apparently, as the title of one work claims, *It feels good to forgive*.[10] Morally, it builds character and contributes to overall emotional maturity.[11] Forgiveness appears to be so effective for such a wide range of problems that it is even being considered as an empirically supported treatment—the title coveted by those who present new interventions, as such treatments are usually accompanied by increased third-party reimbursements.[12] Robert D. Enright confidently states that "forgiveness works."[13] Yet some are concerned that the benefits of forgiveness have been exaggerated. Jeffrie G. Murphy wonders if forgiveness is becoming a "universal panacea for all mental, moral, and spiritual ills."[14] Despite these questions, there is some evidence from the current research that forgiveness is good for us.

If emphasizing the positive does not work, a corollary of this kind of research is that *not* forgiving is *bad* for us. Not only does it increase the chances for ulcers, high blood pressure, and ostensibly, all of the other disorders that forgiveness would help alleviate; but it also allows anger to fester, thereby causing all kinds of additional damage. Some authors compare unforgiveness to the "fight or flight" mechanism in that it serves well as a self-protective measure for a very short time, but no human was meant to live in that state permanently.[15] Others equate unforgiveness with anger and thus emphasize forgiveness as a useful way to reduce all of the potential harm that can come from suppressed resentment.[16] Hence, if unforgiveness promotes emotional conditions that have already been shown to be dysfunctional, then any intervention that reduces or eliminates such symptoms would clearly be healthy and beneficial. Thus, as an antidote to all of the toxic side effects of unforgiveness, some kind of forgiveness procedure seems to fit the bill nicely.

Factors That Correlate with Forgiveness

Another major theme of the research goes this way: since forgiveness is so good, it must be advantageous to identify factors that help or hinder the act of forgiveness. Anyone familiar with psychological theory will recognize the various attachment styles usually formed early in life and used as relational templates from then on. It should come as no surprise that those with secure attachment styles seem to have an easier time with forgiveness. In addition, certain personality traits and conflict resolution styles also correlate with a greater ability to forgive. These are just some of the variables that positively correlate with forgiveness, while, not surprisingly, rumination or brooding does not correlate as highly.

Design of Forgiveness Assessment Tools

A third conclusion from current research is that the newly discovered power of forgiveness has spawned a new cottage industry—the creation of assessment tools for measuring a person's level of forgiveness.[17] These scales, in typical research fashion, assign a numerical value to either someone's level of forgiveness or her propensity to forgive. Again, if forgiveness is beneficial, it is incumbent upon researchers and counselors to be able to assess whether and to what degree clients are correctly performing such a powerful technique. There are at least two counseling related concerns with these tools aside from the diversity of definitions of forgiveness.[18] First, the designer of the scale must assign some kind of quantitative threshold as a target for the client to reach. This could create pressure on the client to aim for a particular score rather than struggle with what forgiveness might mean in her particular situation. The second concern is the fact that this kind of research can only provide a snapshot of where the client might be in a specific moment in time. Where she is on a trajectory might be harder to measure (repeated administrations of the same test risk being corrupted by practice effect). If the process of forgiveness is often a winding road with lots of turns, the value of measuring one particular location is questionable.

Construction of Forgiveness Models

The final theme of contemporary forgiveness literature which can aid us in defining forgiveness is the actual methodology—a "how-to manual," essentially. This is the most theoretical of the four themes and thus not technically research in the purest sense of the word. Not surprisingly, for this reason and others, the conclusions about how to do forgiveness are varied; to date, there are close to twenty different step-by-step models. A cursory study noting the number of steps required to forgive (average of five, with a standard deviation of two) reveals the wide diversity. One method advocates as many as sixteen steps! Can all of these recipes possibly produce the same dish?

ASSESSING TWO COMMON FORGIVENESS MODELS

Although each model has its own distinctive formula, surveying two of the more dominant paradigms of how to carry out forgiveness will at least provide some sense of what is usually portrayed as forgiveness. These are Enright's four-phase model and Everett L. Worthington's five-step model.[19] Because these are two of the shorter models, many of the concepts mentioned are expanded upon in the other models. A comparison of these two models gives a sense of how the various models relate. The following chart outlines the two models and shows where they overlap.

Enright	Worthington
Uncovering the Anger	Recall the Hurt
	Empathizing with the Offender
Deciding to Forgive	Altruistic Gift of Forgiveness
Working on Forgiving	Commit Publicly to Forgive
	Hold onto Forgiveness
Discovery and Release	

Enright

Enright's four-phase model is actually much more involved than just four discrete steps; there are several subpoints under each phase. The first phase, Uncovering the Anger, assumes that the victim is repressing or denying the appropriate anger related to the offense. The anger eating away at the victim is what causes so many of the injurious side effects mentioned above. In Enright's model, "unforgiveness" is another term for anger, specifically unresolved anger. If this anger is not faced squarely, no real forgiveness can occur. Like spoiled food, it must be expunged in order for the body to feel better. Denying the poison only makes things worse.

Once the anger has been faced and released to some degree, the potential forgiver next needs to decide to forgive. The implication here is that if the victim makes the decision, it is more likely to be real and therefore completed. A person rarely does something without first deciding to do it. The actual decision somehow reduces ambivalence and anxiety. Deciding to forgive (especially after the anger has run its course) is similar.

Curiously, somewhere between Steps 2 and 3, actual forgiveness takes place. By Step 3 the forgiver is "working on" following through with the decision of Step 2. Forgiveness can be hard work and thus continual reinforcement may be needed to make forgiveness feel real. Although the model does not spell out when this actually happens, it is eventually cause for joy. An emerging recognition on the part of the victim that she has indeed forgiven her offender brings a new sense of relief. Those negative side effects that come with unforgiveness evaporate, while all of the positive blessings that accompany forgiveness emerge.

Worthington

Worthington's model begins similarly, although he broadens the emotional response to involve recalling the hurt. This hurt may include anger but is not limited to it. Feelings of sadness, betrayal, pain, and many other emotions must be faced openly and honestly. Again, to deny the pain (in whatever form) only makes things worse.

At this point Worthington inserts a second preliminary step before the actual step of forgiveness: Empathizing with the Offender, in which empathy means the victim imagines herself in the shoes of the offender. "Why did he do it? How intentional was it? How could I, if I were he, ever do such a thing?" are all questions victims should explore as they attempt to project themselves into the minds of the offenders. The assumption here is that to whatever degree the victim can empathize at all with the offender, forgiveness will come that much more easily. This step comes before the actual step of forgiveness because it provides the victim a bridge from thinking of her own pain (Step 1: Recall the Hurt) to thinking of the pain of the offender, which eventually leads to forgiving him. The victim first embraces her own pain and is prepared through this empathy to feel the pain of the offender, which in turn paves the way for forgiveness.

Worthington's decision step is framed in terms of an altruistic gift to the offender. Since presumably the victim has already made the switch in her mind from thinking of her own pain to thinking of the pain of the offender, the forgiveness is free ("a gift") and for his sake. It is this supposed "other-centeredness" that makes the decision possible, but it is still a *decision* to forgive—which remains undefined. Like Enright, Worthington does not include a step that explains or describes the actual forgiveness and therefore, we are left to assume that it occurs somewhere between Steps 3 and 4.

Following such a decision to forgive, there is often a great deal of residual pain and resentment. Worthington explains this as the emotions not keeping up with the will. In other words, we can decide to forgive (and presumably even do it) and still not "feel" like everything has been resolved. One of the ways to accelerate this reuniting of the emotions with the will is to commit publicly to forgive. It is as if the will says to the emotions, "We are now going on the public record with this decision, so you had better catch up." Going public with a decision makes reneging just a little bit more difficult (although not impossible). Even after a public pronouncement, a gap can still exist between what a person has done and how she feels about the whole situation. For some people forgiveness is hard and long and thus has to be "worked through" (Step 5).

From this brief survey of two dominant views of forgiveness, it is clear that models may overlap at some points, and yet, there are significant differences. For example, Enright makes anger the main emotion that needs to be faced, whereas Worthington broadens it to hurt. Worthington adds the step of empathy as preliminary to the actual decision to forgive, whereas Enright moves directly from facing anger to deciding to forgive. Finally, Enright's model ends with a sense of joy and release, but Worthington leaves his forgivers still struggling to hold on to whatever forgiveness they were able to muster. These divergences, revealed in a comparison of just two of the shorter models, multiply in examinations of the longer models of forgiveness.

If the major models cannot provide coherent definitions of forgiveness, is there any hope for a universal definition? Although a great deal of measuring is being done by those conducting empirical forgiveness researches, the theoretical foundation (from which any ultimate definition must be derived) is lagging behind. Worthington even laments that "one important yet unresolved conceptual issue is the definition of forgiveness."[20] Others also concede that no "gold standard" or "consensual definition" of forgiveness exists.[21] Some forgiveness writers assume such familiarity on the part of their readers that they never even attempt to define the word.[22] Another way some authors attempt to bring clarity is to prefix the term with an adjective. One attempt to provide a forgiveness classification scheme is that given by F. LeRon Shults and Steven J. Sandage, who identify at least three types of forgiveness: *therapeutic, forensic,* and *relational.*[23]

FORGIVENESS TAXONOMY

Therapeutic Forgiveness

The first and most common type of forgiveness is *therapeutic* forgiveness. As the name implies, this type of forgiveness is concerned primarily with the healing power of forgiveness *for the victim.* Those who are wounded at the hands of others often continue to suffer emotional discomfort long after the sin has been perpetrated. While therapeutic forgiveness may have some healthful benefit if practiced immediately, it is more often advocated as a balm for the wound of ingrained resentment that refuses to heal itself over time. This raw sore of toxic, slow-burning anger needs to be lanced so healing can finally occur. Whatever forgiveness means, it eventually leads to some kind of resolution in the mind of the victim whereby neither the original offense nor the subsequent resentment can cause any fresh pain. Because forgiveness is presented as a remedy for resentment, many forgiveness writers equate forgiveness and healing.

Lewis B. Smedes clearly advocates for this position,[24] and he is usually cited as a spokesperson for this type of forgiveness.[25] Echoing Smedes, the majority of contemporary forgiveness researchers, in their attempts to identify and measure the benefits of forgiveness, work from the same basic framework. If there are clear beneficial side effects for those who can manage somehow to forgive, it behooves a victim to forgive in order to experience these benefits. Indeed, the promise of feeling better has become the primary market strategy for forgiveness. The more the benefits of forgiveness are identified, the more a person should *want* to forgive so as to reap these rewards. Whether it is appropriate or morally defensible to forgive in a particular situation is not the point. Since it is in the victim's *best interest* to forgive, she should go ahead and do it (definitional ambiguity aside). In other words, the primary motivation for forgiveness becomes either to reap the benefits of forgiveness (it is good for me) or to eliminate the negative side effects of not forgiving (unforgiveness is bad for me).

Concerns with Therapeutic Forgiveness

There are at least three concerns with this type of forgiveness. The first concern is that if personal healing becomes the primary objective, forgiveness can too easily be seen as a means to an end rather than as an end itself; that is, forgiveness becomes a path to emotional, physical, and even spiritual wholeness rather than a remedy for sin, as it is presented in Scripture and Christian theology. If it is merely a non-theologically driven psychological technique, then it can be employed in multiple settings (even non-Christian) and the outcomes measured. If this intervention proves to be statistically successful, it could even be elevated to that coveted category—empirically supported treatments—as some are even now advocating.[26] It is not unrealistic to predict that if present trends continue, one day soon insurance companies will pay for some kind of forgiveness therapy as a proven treatment for a multitude of emotional ills.

The question is, will the forgiveness reimbursed by the insurance companies in any way resemble the forgiveness taught in Scripture? Nigel Biggar points out that the ultimate result of viewing forgiveness primarily through a therapeutic lens is that forgiveness becomes more materialistic and less theological.[27] He cites Worthington's emphasis on the relationship between the "fight or flight" mechanism and the "neurobiological foundation" of forgiveness (in contrast to the relatively little said by Worthington about the theological foundations of forgiveness) as evidence of this reductionist trend.[28] For example, Biggar mentions a book edited by Worthington,[29] in which the portion of the book devoted to psychological research on forgiveness clearly overshadows the one chapter addressing theological perspectives.

In contrast to Worthington and others, Katheryn Rhoads Meek and Mark R. McMinn[30] warn of at least two dangers in ignoring the biblically and theologically rich roots of forgiveness to pursue some short-term therapeutic gain. First, because the precedent for human forgiveness is divine forgiveness, the victim must face the universal brokenness that comes with a biblical view of sin. Facing another's sin always involves a fresh opportunity to look at the victim's own failings. This insight cannot come except and until the victim sees that depravity has cursed all and that none really deserves God's grace. However, once the victim tastes God's unmerited favor, she is in a position to "lovingly identify" with her offenders and see them holistically rather than just view them as people who wronged her. In other words, forgiveness helps us grow in empathy as well as insight, so if we ignore the biblical data on forgiveness, *we as victims* will be worse off (i.e., less insightful and less empathic). The deeper reason, however, why the scriptural teaching on forgiveness cannot be ignored, is that when we forgive, we are modeling God. Therefore, failure to embrace true biblical forgiveness would not be honoring to Him.*

Meek and McMinn's points are a helpful corrective to the materialistic view of forgiveness typically presented, but even their approach focuses on the advantages and disadvantages of forgiveness *for the victim* and thus it is similar to the basic tenet of therapeutic forgiveness in which the victim will benefit from forgiving (or lose out by not forgiving).

A second and not totally unrelated concern with therapeutic forgiveness is that it often reinforces the victim's tendency to focus on herself and her pain, prompting a primarily self-motivated demand for healing. Those who see forgiveness as more of a virtue than a clinical intervention are troubled by the potential self-centeredness of therapeutic forgiveness.[31] Apparently, God's only role in this drama is to facilitate the healing, while the offender need not play any role whatsoever. The victim becomes preoccupied with her own discomfort and thus risks a self-absorption that eventually becomes addictive. In contrast, many of the most moving stories about forgiveness in Scripture involve the rich blessing that forgiveness is *to the offender*.

Indeed, God is the most common forgiver in Scripture. More passages refer to God's forgiveness of humans than to humans' forgiveness of each other. Clearly, His forgiveness brings with it incredible riches *for the forgiven*. For example, Psalm 32:1 claims, "*Blessed* is the man whose sin is forgiven" (emphasis added). Here it is the *forgiven one* (i.e., the offender) who is described as blessed, not the forgiver. This is not to say that God derives no pleasure or subjective benefit from forgiving His

---

* This will be the subject of Chapter 4.

wayward people. It was, after all, for the *joy* that was set before Him that He endured the cross (Heb. 12:2), and the heavenly Shepherd experiences great delight when one of His wayward sheep is found (Luke 15:1–7). However, the overwhelming beneficiaries of God's forgiveness are those who receive it. God's forgiveness, in contrast to therapeutic forgiveness, is other-centered. To put it another way, God does not forgive so that He can get a good night's sleep.

A final concern, and the one mentioned by Shults and Sandage, is that therapeutic forgiveness tends to marginalize the relational aspects of forgiveness.[32] Since the primary goal of therapeutic forgiveness is healing for the victim, the relationship with the offender becomes almost irrelevant. As image-bearers of a triune God, we were created for relationship, first with God and then with each other. We are not relationally autonomous but rather derivative. Thus, we more fully live out our created destiny to the degree that we are connected with each other.[33] Part of this connection is to become practiced at forgiving one another.

Forensic Forgiveness

Therapeutic forgiveness, as its label implies, is usually advocated in the domain of psychology and psychotherapy, whereas the second type of forgiveness listed by Shults and Sandage, namely *forensic* forgiveness, more commonly relates to issues of theology. This kind of forgiveness usually involves the metaphor of paying the price for sin, whether in the legal realm or in the marketplace. With its theological emphasis, it is this type of forgiveness that is typically associated with Christian orthodoxy.

Concerns with Forensic Forgiveness

One of the major themes of Shults and Sandage's book, however, is that to give the forensic aspects of forgiveness primary or foundational explanatory power is to severely limit the relational and interpersonal richness that is just as important to a fuller understanding of forgiveness. Forensic forgiveness is limited to a "transaction . . . in which one party agrees not to exact what the law requires,"[34] followed by the warning not to stretch the metaphor too far.[35] The question is never asked, "Why is the demand for punishment dropped?" or "Why is the debt cancelled?" By ignoring this question, Shults and Sandage somehow use both the illustrations of a child petulantly mouthing words while storming off and of nations forgiving other nations' debts as two examples of the same semantic field.[36]

Several additional questions are relevant to Shults and Sandage's understanding of forensic forgiveness. First, does the Bible support such a limited view of forgiveness—one that only sees forgiveness as some kind of legal transaction? Since Shults and Sandage link traditional theological understandings of forgiveness with this category, is this a legitimate characterization of the historical, evangelical understanding of forgiveness in the first place? And finally, to the degree that the authors have constructed a straw man of forensic forgiveness, are they risking creating more problems than they are attempting to solve by "revising" or "improving on" traditional understandings of forgiveness? While defining forgiveness in *exclusively* forensic terms is obviously reductionistic, diminishing the forensic elements of forgiveness seems a lot worse. The authors conclude, "All of this suggests that salvation is about more than a forensic application of forgiveness."[37] Of course it is about more, but is it ever about less?

Relational Forgiveness

The third option cited by Shults and Sandage (and their preference) is *relational* forgiveness. This definition presumes all of the orthodoxy of forensic forgiveness but deliberately emphasizes the interpersonal experience involved during a rupture and possible reconciliation of a relationship. As the authors put it, "The New Testament *occasionally* uses penal and financial metaphors for salvation, especially in the context of parables, but as we shall see, the *overarching* meaning of forgiveness is manifesting and sharing redemptive grace. In Christian theology, salvation is about grace."[38] Of course, this construal presupposes the restricted definition of forensic forgiveness mentioned above. A broader (and more biblical) definition of forensic forgiveness would still emphasize the foundational aspects of the transaction but also recognize that any such transaction is between people and thus the relational elements can never be excluded.

Other Types of Forgiveness

There are other categories of forgiveness mentioned in the literature. One type frequently championed is that which consists exclusively of activity by the victim. Almost all contemporary therapeutic forgiveness writers celebrate that this powerful intervention is wholly within the power of the victim alone. Thus, the lack of participation on the part of the perpetrator is no threat to the process. Waiting for the offender to repent (or be involved at all) only restores to the offender power that the victim can possess through forgiveness. Most of the forgiveness authors sing the praises of this method of forgiveness, but it was a pastor/theologian who accurately coined the term "unilateral forgiveness."[39] Although the source of the wound may be *interpersonal*, the healing which comes through forgiveness does not necessarily have to be; it can be purely *unilateral*.

Add to this list *dispositional* forgiveness, which characterizes one victim with a forgiving spirit, in contrast to another who is able to practice *situational* (specific event) forgiveness,[40] and the labels go on and on. But does adding an adjective to the term "forgiveness" resolve the problem of definition issues? It does not help much if the adjective is clearer than the noun it is modifying. What if we are clear about terms like "unilateral," "therapeutic," "forensic," and other modifiers, but still do not understand forgiveness itself? The definition becomes even more clouded when two opposing adjectives are used to describe the same construct. For instance, how can forgiveness be both unilateral and interpersonal at the same time? How can the offender be involved and not involved at the same time?

To use a biblical example, when did the father *actually forgive* his wayward son (Luke 15:1–32)? Was it when he saw his son coming down the road? Was it in response to his son's repentance speech (vs. 21)? If so, this would be an example of *interpersonal* forgiveness—a *transaction between* the father and the son. But what if the father forgave the son long before, maybe even as the son was leaving? This type of forgiveness would be *unilateral* as it did not involve any action on the part of the son at all. Is the term "forgiveness" broad enough to include the father's loving attitude toward his son as he was leaving *and* his restoring response upon his return?*

---

* Of course, it must be remembered that the story of the prodigal son is not an allegory but rather a parable Jesus told to make one primary point: God experiences joy when that which was lost is found. Therefore, care must be exercised before interpreting every detail of the story. I only use it here because it is frequently referenced by forgiveness writers and to illustrate the point about the diversity of forgiveness definitions.

With the diversity of forgiveness definitions, are we as Christians free to pick and choose the definition that suits us or works for us? Has forgiveness become a vague inkblot onto which we project our own idiosyncratic meaning? For a Christian, this is not an option. Whatever forgiveness means, it must be first rooted in Scripture and Christian theology, its original home before current research discovered it. Additionally, because forgiveness is an imperative for believers, God must have had something in mind when He commanded it.

In the case of George and Ellen mentioned earlier, it is obvious that they are guilty of a great deal of sin against one another. In light of the current confusion over what forgiveness means, we can perhaps at least excuse their lack of clarity and consistency concerning forgiveness. But this still does not absolve them of the call to forgive one another. As a counselor I must help them negotiate a more accurate and meaningful definition of forgiveness so when they actually do forgive one another, it will have more substance and permanence.

CHAPTER 2

SHARPENING THE DEFINITION OF FORGIVENESS

Little theory has been advanced about unforgiveness and forgiveness.

—Everett L. Worthington, Jr.

In the rush to measure the different aspects of forgiveness, research findings have outpaced theoretical definitions. We may know, for example, that people with a certain temperament report that it is easy or common for them to forgive. However, we are not sure what they are claiming is easier to do. Researchers recognize this problem of definition. Some are content to offer no definition and let the subjects define forgiveness for themselves under the assumption that everyone has some idea about forgiveness and those ideas overlap enough to measure. Yet the standard rules of research demand operationalized definitions (terms constructed in such a way that we can *do* something with them and get the same results, or in laymen's terms, reduce constructs to numbers). Consequently, most researchers construct their own idiosyncratic definitions of forgiveness and then conduct their research accordingly. These studies are accumulated together as forgiveness research. Of course the problem with this method is that each researcher is potentially dealing with a slightly, or sometimes significantly, different construct and this limits their studies only to those who forgive their way. If there is more or less to forgiveness than what a particular researcher has indicated, this part of the definition gets missed. To complicate matters further, there is some question as to whether the more popular research definitions of forgiveness even represent the views of most non-researchers.[1]

Most definitions of forgiveness are meant to provide clarity and understanding rather than to be used as research constructs. However, these definitions often struggle with saying too much or too little. There are advantages to having a simple sound bite definition. It clarifies forgiveness into one basic idea and clears the way for action. For example, Smedes defines forgiveness as merely being willing to use "magic eyes," a reference to his allegory about the man dealing with his wife's adultery.[2] To those unfamiliar with the story, the husband in Smedes' book resolutely determines to view his wife as if she had never been unfaithful and conducts their marriage accordingly. This is similar to the idea that forgiveness is "letting go of the need for vengeance and releasing negative thoughts of bitterness and resentment,"[3] or briefer yet, forgiveness is merely "giving up one's right to hurt back."[4]

The problem, of course, with such pithy descriptions of forgiveness is that they are too simple. Questions arise, such as, just *how* do I let go of the need for vengeance? Or release negative thoughts? And is vengeance actually needed anyway? Where do all of these negative thoughts come from? And are the negative thoughts really the core of the problem? If I really have a *right* to hurt back, why should I give that up? And finally, where do I obtain that pair of "magic eyes"?

To avoid the simplicity of the briefer definitions, some forgiveness writers attempt to construct a comprehensive definition that answers all of the questions in one long, drawn-out, sentence:

> People, upon rationally determining that they have been unfairly treated, forgive when they willfully abandon resentment and related responses (to which they have a right), and endeavor to respond to the wrong-doer based on the moral principle of beneficence, which may include compassion, unconditional worth, generosity and moral love (to which the wrongdoer, by nature of the hurtful act or acts, has no right).[5]

This definition requires the reader to keep several thoughts in mind as each new aspect of the definition is added. The victims must first determine whether an injustice has occurred and then recognize that the feelings of resentment are appropriate *but* must be willingly abandoned (whatever that means), *and then* the victims must go on to treat their offenders in accordance with goodwill, all the while recognizing that the offenders have no intrinsic right to such treatment. In other words, the victims give up their rights and offenders receive what they have no right to receive.

Definitions like this do answer some of the questions left out of the sound bites, but even with multiple words and phrases, they still do not actually define forgiveness. For example, the above definition, apart from all of the disclaimers and conditions, really boils down to forgiveness being equated with choosing not to be angry with the offender and treating the offender kindly. Is there no more to forgiveness than this? Forgiveness may be a little easier to define with the addition of boundaries around the construct. Identifying at least some of what does *not* count as forgiveness may not result in the absolute definition, but could provide some limits within which to work.

THREE BOUNDARIES AROUND THE CONSTRUCT OF FORGIVENESS

This chapter will identify three boundaries around the construct of forgiveness and then introduce four definitional contours of forgiveness from a Christian perspective. The first boundary restricts the situations that warrant forgiveness. The second boundary distinguishes forgiveness from a cognitive reframe. Finally, the third boundary clarifies the relationship between forgiveness and empathy.

Boundary #1: Forgiveness Is a Response to a Moral Violation

Forgiveness, in order to make sense, must presuppose that an *offense* has been committed; otherwise there would be nothing to forgive. Imagine the following conversation:

"Missed you at the coffee shop last night."
"Really? I didn't know we were even meeting last night."
"Of course we were. I texted you three times. Maybe you should

check your phone more often. Oh, well, it's no big deal. I forgive you. I'll contact you about our next meeting."

Something does not sound right about this interchange. Forgiving a friend for not checking her phone several times a day seems a little extreme. Forgiveness seems out of place here because it is usually related to an offense, that is, a moral violation (or at least a perception of a moral violation). Other virtues like tolerance, forbearance, and patience involve dealing with our disappointment or disagreement with others, but we reserve forgiveness for those who have *morally* offended us. Thus, forgiveness is inappropriate in the case of a misunderstanding. One of the earliest pioneers of the current research on forgiveness makes this point:

> If we understand why someone did what he did, we do not forgive him. We forgive him only when we cannot understand why he did it. If we really understood why someone had to hurt us, we would know he could not help himself and we would excuse him instead of blame him. And if we excuse someone, we do not need to forgive him because we only forgive the ones we blame.[6]

Similarly, in Scripture, God only forgives those who have committed moral violations against Him. We are instructed to confess our sins (1 John 1:9), not our stupidity, clumsiness, or lack of knowledge. God does not forgive misunderstandings; He only forgives sin. One major difference, of course, is that in God's case the subjective element (mistaking something as a moral violation when it is not) does not apply, for His assessment of that which is moral and that which is immoral is always accurate. In other words, God forgives sin as He accurately defines it.

If this is true, there are several other situations in which forgiveness is inappropriate. Mere disagreement, if there is no sin involved, does not warrant forgiveness. For example, we do not usually forgive someone for holding a different viewpoint or voting differently than we do. Neither do we forgive someone for beating us in golf or chess (pride might need to be addressed, but that is a different issue).

Putting this limitation on what counts as forgiveness provides some structure for our definition. In other words, anything other than a moral violation requires something other than forgiveness. Therefore, responses given in reaction to something other than a moral violation do not count as forgiveness. If forgiveness is only appropriate in response to a moral violation, it cannot be synonymous with condoning, for condoning changes the offense of the original violation into something less offensive (or not offensive at all). And if the offense or violation is reconfigured to be other than a moral violation, then forgiveness is no longer necessary in the first place.

So before considering forgiveness, the victim must ask if a moral violation has actually occurred and if so, identify the violation. This discussion over what counts as sin and what does not may seem a bit too detailed, but it is nonetheless important because of the difference between the responses to sin and those to misunderstanding. Although we tend to feel shame as an appropriate response to sinful behavior, we also feel shame in other situations where it may not be warranted. In fact, many times we feel shame for what is not innately dishonorable (i.e., clumsiness) and feel less shame for what is really disgraceful. For example, which usually brings on a greater sense of shame: accidentally spilling coffee on someone's new outfit or spreading rumors about him clandestinely? Which event would generate an apology more quickly?

Restricting forgiveness to an appropriate response to moral violations helps to provide one boundary around the construct, and results in at least one implication. The implication of this boundary is that any resolution (including forgiveness) of a moral violation must be morally defensible. Thus, when we forgive, it must be for a morally justifiable reason.

Boundary #2: Forgiveness Is Not a Cognitive Reframe

Cognitive reframing is a classic therapeutic technique to get clients to view their struggles differently and thus infuse hope where disillusion and maybe depression held sway. The theory (appropriately named *cognitive behaviorism*) teaches that if people can see things differently (through magic eyes?), they become free to behave differently. In laymen's terms: If life gives me lemons (usually a type for something sour in our culture), I can see this as an opportunity (cognitive reframe) rather than a curse, and thus I am free to make lemonade (positive behavioral choice).*

---

* This concept, of course, has implications way beyond the counseling room and into the realms of philosophy, epistemology, and even theology. Some believe that there is no reality except

Cognitive behavioral counselors have noticed how perception shapes behavior and have used it as a tool to decrease resentment in their clients. For example, how does a woman view her husband who is addicted to Internet pornography? Is he a pervert? Is he sexually frustrated or crying out for a deeper connection with his wife? Does he suffer from an addictive personality or was he sexually abused as a child? As a male in our society, is he a victim of the seductive visual images omnipresent in our culture? Each of these explanations will not only affect how the wife views her husband but will also, to a great extent, shape her behavioral response to him.*

So which explanation(s) should the wife embrace (and the therapist encourage)? It depends on her goal. If the goal is for the wife to feel more positive about her husband and thus be willing to work on their marriage again, an account that frames his behavior as a cry for intimacy with her would surely be more attractive than viewing him as a sexual predator. The short-term advantage to this approach is a temporary reduction in the resentment and a window of opportunity to work on the marriage. The disadvantage is that in her attempt to see things in a way that leads to positive feelings, she may miss what is actually true about her husband. Suppose he is not crying out for more intimacy with her but is rather acting out his lifelong hatred toward women. Her movement toward him in that case only makes her more vulnerable.

When it comes to forgiveness, most contemporary definitions seem to be some version of a cognitive reframe. Aside from the fact that the majority of lay people (people not involved in producing forgiveness research) intuitively disagree with this characterization,[7] there are three more concerns with defining forgiveness as a cognitive reframe. First, this definition blurs the line between forgiveness and other related concepts such as condoning, excusing, justifying, or showing mercy, all of which do include some kind of rethinking or revising of a previously held view. For example, if after reflection, the victim somehow reduces

---

that which we construct; others believe there is a reality but it is inescapably shaped by our construction of it. Finally, there are those who believe there is a 1:1 correspondence between reality and how we perceive it. For the purposes of constructing a Christian definition of forgiveness, discussion will be limited to the therapeutic and the theological.

* I realize that human behavior is most often multi-causal and so to frame the question in terms of the *one reason* is admittedly reductionistic. The point is to show that how a person views (or chooses to view) an offense has a great deal of impact on how she responds.

the offense (cognitively reframing the sin from "really bad" to "kind of bad"), she is actually condoning what was done. This might be appropriate if her reassessment is correct, but regardless, condoning necessarily reduces the need for forgiveness. Likewise, if she recognizes factors about her offender that modify the crime, she is excusing, *not* forgiving. Also, there are times when she will revise her assessment and conclude that what her offender did was somehow actually right, that is, justified. In this case, forgiveness is inappropriate because there is nothing left to forgive. Finally, the victim may just choose, for whatever reason, to treat her offender in a way that is less harsh than warranted. Showing mercy, however, is not the same as forgiveness.[8]

The second concern about the cognitive reframe view of forgiveness is that the victim may actually end up distorting reality. What if the victim is correct in her assessment that a true violation did indeed occur? If forgiveness requires some kind of restructuring of reality, is she not being asked to suspend her sense of what is true? Alistair McFadyen asks this pointed question, "Does forgiveness enact a truthful relationship to the past—rather than covering it over, laying aside and forgetting it?"[9] How must the adult man interpret his father's violent abuse of him as a boy? Did it really happen? Was it really that bad? Did his father just not know any better? Again, McFadyen wonders if Christianity "obliges victims to instantaneous and unconditional forgiveness, where forgiveness is a kind of forgetting—acting as though no wrong had been done—which also involves a letting go of the truth of the situation."[10] In other words, must truth be sacrificed (by means of a cognitive reframe) on the altar of forgiveness?

The third concern with the cognitive reframe view of forgiveness is related to the second. If this kind of reality reconstruction is done enough, the victim learns to mistrust her own appraisals of people and situations. When her internal radar is always being ignored or the data supplied by her radar is constantly being corrected, eventually she will begin to wonder if she can ever see things close to how they really are.* This could lead to an unhealthy dependence on others to define and interpret reality for her, which in the long run only makes her *more*

---

* Again, I recognize that everybody's radar is broken to some degree. In a fallen world, we cannot afford to merely "trust our gut." However, I think that consistently discrediting our sense of being violated only degrades our radar further.

vulnerable to future abuse, not less. It is as if her early warning system has been dismantled due to poor performance.*

For example, with no visible sign of discomfort, Carla plainly informed me that her uncle did indeed engage in sexual activity with her when she was a child. However, she was quick to add that his behavior was understandable in light of the fact that she ran around in front of him in her bathing suit and therefore somehow tempted him; at least, that is her uncle's story and he is sticking to it. Since she had been warned in church about the effect women's immodest attire can have on men, she admitted that she should have known that she was being seductive. Of course she neglected to mention that *her memory* of these events is very different from that of her uncle. What *she* remembered was an initial desire for closeness with her uncle followed by a deep sense of violation. She had no recollection of being seductive as a seven-year-old girl, just a sense of innocence that has been replaced by a cynicism that often borders on depression. So what really happened? If her uncle was merely overwhelmed by her emerging toxic femininity, then something is seriously wrong *with her*. Furthermore, if her radar keeps triggering, warning her of external threats when the real problem is with her, then something is wrong with her radar. Like a smoke alarm that keeps going off at the wrong time, eventually the temptation to remove the batteries becomes irresistible.

This is why regular repentance and confession are so important, especially in relationships. Our spouses, families, and friends *know* (both theologically and experientially) that we are sinners and sin against them. When we violate them, their radars send off warnings indicating a wrong has been committed. But if confrontation consistently leads to denial, excusing, condoning, or justifying (pressures to cognitively reframe the situation), not only are we defending our behavior in the short term but we are also planting in our victims' minds the long-term seed of distrust in their own radar systems. After a while, it is tempting for them to conclude that with abysmal track records ("I think I was sinned against but I guess I was not"), their radars must be broken. If their radars are broken,

---

* I believe this partly explains why sexual abuse victims often get re-abused. Their early warning systems have been severely degraded through constant pressure to reframe the incoming danger signals.

they become even more vulnerable not only to our sin but also to the sin of others. Confession and repentance, on the other hand, assure that a victim's radar is functioning at least reasonably well and thus actually contributes to a more robust defense in the future.

Boundary #3: Forgiveness Is More Than Empathy

If a moral offense has indeed occurred and it cannot be cognitively restructured away, then how are victims to deal with the bad feelings? Many forgiveness authors suggest some kind of empathy with the perpetrator as a means of ameliorating the resentment. Recall that Worthington makes empathy a prerequisite (Step 2) to the decision (Step 3) to forgive, almost as if empathy initiates a momentum that concludes with forgiveness. This can be either the result of theological reflection or an imaginative exercise.

Theologically, every victim is also a perpetrator of something. To use biblical language, there is none righteous and we all (victims and perpetrators alike) stand in need of God's forgiveness and grace. Since we want to be forgiven for our sin, should we not offer that forgiveness to others? Even the Lord's Prayer seems to support this relationship by linking God's forgiveness of us (which we need and long for) with our forgiveness of others. Since we are not innocent and yet desire pardon (and have received it), should we not extend that pardon to those who hurt us? Do those that wrong us not long to be forgiven just as we do? When we look into our offender's eyes (as did Simon Wiesenthal with a Nazi war criminal),[11] do we not see the same offensive darkness that we know to be inside us? Unless we are comfortable with a view that categorizes levels of sin, we are both equally guilty. The bottom line is, how can we resent our offenders in light of our own sin, which is equally worthy of God's resentment? This particular theological issue will be addressed later but for now it is enough to make the point that if the victim's sin cancels out the sin of the perpetrator, then the whole basis for justice collapses. If we are always guilty in some kind of morally equivalent way, then we can never charge our offenders. If a victim must be totally free of any sinful behaviors or thoughts before the offender can be addressed, justice would never occur. In the classic passage on confronting a brother (Matt. 18:15–20), the victim's sin (which we know is present from the rest of Scripture) is never mentioned.

The second way to generate empathy for our offenders is to imagine ourselves in their place and feel what they feel. What were they thinking when they did this to me? What was going on in their lives? What were they struggling with? Could there be something about their story that would make some kind of sense of their behavior? Whether the metaphor is to walk in the offender's shoes or see the world through the offender's eyes, empathy involves a willingness to identify with the feelings of the offender, and this identification somehow changes the way in which victims view the situation.

Perhaps the reason that forgiveness writers advocate this exercise of empathy is that the result will almost always be a little less resentment toward the perpetrator. But why is this? Part of the reason is that I can never truly see things through someone else's eyes. Coupled with whatever accurate insights into my offender's experience I may be able to glean are my own *projections* onto him of what I would be thinking *were I in his place.* The question then must be asked, is projecting *me* onto *him* really true empathy?

For example, I hear of a robbery on the news and I attempt to put myself in the robber's shoes. The only reason I can think of to rob someone would be to get money for an emergency. Thus there must be some pressure in the robber's life that led him to his crime. While I cannot sympathize with the criminal activity, I can perhaps in some way understand why he might have done it. Just this mental exercise alone has resulted in my being a little less upset with the robber for stealing. Can this kind of empathy ever be otherwise? Since when I look at my own sin, I typically give myself a great deal of latitude, would it not be consistent that when I project myself onto others, I extend to them the same latitude? This kind of empathic bond with my offender actually cuts us both some slack.

Empathy leads to reducing resentment in one of two ways. Either I look at the situation theologically and conclude we are both guilty, or I look at the situation circumstantially and conclude that neither one of us is really that bad. Either way, there is a leveling of moral guilt which understandably results in a little less resentment toward the perpetrator on the part of the victim. If resentment is most often seen as the root of all evil, then to reduce resentment by any means is seen as a good thing. But the question must be asked again, is restructuring the truth too high a price to pay for reducing resentment?

Four Contours of a Christian Approach to Forgiveness

With at least these three boundaries in place—forgiveness is only appropriate in response to sin, it is not a cognitive reframe, and it is not the same as empathy—I believe there are four key questions that must be addressed if a biblical definition of forgiveness is to be gained. Each of these questions will be addressed individually in detail later. I introduce them at this point to illustrate how they all fit together.

Establishing a biblically supportable definition of forgiveness is not as simple as it may appear. Word studies of the Hebrew and Greek words for forgiveness provide some initial semantic boundaries. However, since words do not occur in a vacuum, an analysis of the context is also required to determine the most accurate meaning. Specific issues must be noted, such as: Who is being forgiven? Who is doing the forgiving? What, if any, are the conditions by which someone may be forgiven? These are all questions that involve more than just a simple definition of the word.

Question #1: How Does God Forgive?

While the mandate to forgive is stated throughout Scripture, there are two key New Testament passages that not only state this mandate, but also provide some clues as to how it is to be done.

> Let all bitterness and wrath and anger and clamor and slander be put away from you, along with all malice. Be kind to one another, tender-hearted, forgiving each other, just as God *in Christ* also has forgiven you (Eph. 4:31–32, emphasis added).

> So, as those who have been chosen by God, holy and beloved, put on a heart of compassion, kindness, humility, gentleness and patience; bearing with one another, and forgiving one another, whoever has a complaint against anyone; *just as the Lord forgave you, so also* should you (Col. 3:12–13, emphasis added).

From these texts, two related parameters for any truly biblical definition of forgiveness can be identified. The first parameter is that human forgiveness should be derived from divine forgiveness, and the second is that all definitions of forgiveness must somehow relate to the gospel

(Christ and His work). Therefore, in order to understand forgiveness from a biblical viewpoint, we must study how God forgives, as well as be well-versed in the gospel.

How God forgives is the subject of Chapter 4, but for now it is enough to state that God *does* have a method or way of forgiving and we are encouraged to model our forgiveness after His. One implication of this position is that we are not at liberty to define forgiveness for ourselves. We are not autonomous in this matter; we are derivative, just as our very nature as God's image-bearers is not autonomous, but rather derivative of God and who He is.

The second parameter is that forgiveness must ultimately be rooted in the gospel. The text does not say that God just arbitrarily forgives. He forgives "in Christ" based on what was accomplished by His Son on the cross. Definitions of the gospel can range from the simple to the complex, but a definition of forgiveness that does not refer back to or emerge from the foundation of the gospel cannot truly be called Christian.

Question #2: How Does Healing Relate to Forgiveness?

Since God, as our model, does not forgive to facilitate any kind of healing for Himself, personal healing cannot be the primary goal of forgiveness. If forgiveness does not facilitate healing, healing must come some other way. Healing can (and usually does) occur apart from any involvement from the offender. Although repentance on the offender's part can play a significant role in healing, it is ultimately not necessary. However, the offender *must* be involved (via repentance) in order for true forgiveness to be offered and received. One implication from these statements is that healing is therefore a prerequisite to and not a result of true forgiveness. A second implication is that if healing comes first, how does it happen?

Question #3: Is Forgiveness Primarily Self-Centered or Other-Centered?

God does not forgive for His sake but rather for the sake of those He is forgiving. Likewise, if we are to model ourselves after Him, our forgiveness must be for the sake of the offender, not for our own pain relief. There are two implications here: The offender must be involved; and repentance (what is in the offender's best interest) must be required.

Question #4: Is Forgiveness Active or Passive?

Forgiveness is not merely a passive "letting go" of some kind of bad feelings, but rather an active, strategic pursuit of the offender for the sake of his well-being and the kingdom of God. The biblical story of Joseph addressed in Chapter 8 is a vivid example of the active nature of true forgiveness.

These four questions will constitute the remainder of this book. But first, it is necessary to address the issue of resentment, since many forgiveness writers target resentment as the main toxic side effect weighing down those who are struggling to forgive.

CHAPTER 3

RESENTMENT AND REPENTANCE

God is a righteous judge, and a God who has indignation every day.

—Psalm 7:11

Interpersonal sin produces uncomfortable emotional side effects. The offense itself hurts, and the subsequent rift in the relationship also causes stress. Forgiveness writers often portray resentment as one of the most dangerous of these residual side effects, which is why most definitions of forgiveness make dealing with resentment either the centerpiece of the definition or at least a key aspect. Why is resentment such a problem when it comes to forgiveness?

David Augsberger surely makes an understatement when he asserts that forgiveness is costly.[1] Even in the rare best-case scenario, in which the offender genuinely repents, there often remains a feeling of relational ambivalence. This struggle with relational ambivalence becomes even more pronounced in the case where there is either no repentance or a disingenuous apology. The forgiveness writers identify these situations as the most difficult for a victim. Indeed, the victim suffers both the damage of the original sin as well as the tension generated by the offender's disavowal of the offense.

The standard advice at this point becomes very equivocal. First, the victim is encouraged to feel everything there is to feel in response to the offense.[2] However, these feelings (especially the negative ones like anger and resentment) are portrayed as having a very short shelf life and will soon spoil. Victims are initially encouraged to embrace strong negative feelings, but shortly thereafter they are warned not to dwell on those feelings. To avoid all of the harmful side effects mentioned earlier, or a "root of bitterness" (Heb. 12:15), these feelings of anger and resentment need to be released before they do permanent damage. The victim is directed to both fully embrace and yet quickly release strong feelings as a step on the way to health. And yet, the standard advice never delineates a point in time when these feelings should be alternately embraced or expunged.

This binge-and-purge approach to dealing with interpersonal sin seems contradictory. Part of this apparent inconsistency may result from a misunderstanding of the internal response that sin against us invokes. Clearly, uncomfortable feelings (for lack of a better term) are generated by others' sin, particularly when there is no repentance. Since these feelings are unpleasant, the assumption is that they are somehow unhealthy and therefore need to be purged. Some forgiveness writers label this response as *resentment* and, consistent with the negative connotations usually associated with the term, pronounce the feelings as harmful, rather than as neutral or even as positive emotions to be explored. In the psychoanalytic tradition, resentment and vindictiveness are sometimes seen as revelatory in that they expose childhood wounds, narcissistic pride, or neurotic envy.[3] Even in these cases, however, the persistence of resentful feelings is still a sign that something is wrong.

At least one writer has attempted to redeem the term "resentment" by portraying it as the most morally responsible (and therefore good and healthy) reaction to evil.*[4] To those who love justice, resentment is a logical and moral response to injustice. To not resent evil is to be apathetic toward it. Thus we should experience an emotionally negative response to sin both in ourselves and in others. If resentment is the correct description of this response, then this resentment is both intrinsically dysfunctional and sinful, or it is actually good and appropriate. Although

---

* I am persuaded by Murphy's arguments and thus I am comfortable using the term "resentment" and/or "vindictiveness" as he does. The reader is free to use a different word if these terms still carry too much negative baggage.

I am comfortable with Jeffrie G. Murphy's use of the term "resentment," for many, the term can never mean anything good. Whether we label this bad feeling as resentment or choose another word for it ("stress," for example, seems too mild), the fact remains that interpersonal sin generates some uncomfortable feelings.

CASCADING LEVELS OF DAMAGE AS A RESULT OF INTERPERSONAL SIN

We must step back to the original offense, in order to discover where this tension originates and what makes interpersonal sin so harmful that residual damage is left even years after the original offense. If someone hurt me in the past and there is little or no chance that it will be repeated, why ruminate on it? Apparently, there must be more damage than that caused by the original violation itself. Enright and other forgiveness writers have identified this secondary damage as *toxic anger.** This constant state of heightened arousal leads to many of the dysfunctional side effects (high blood pressure, difficulty sleeping, reduced immunity, etc.) mentioned earlier that result from unforgiveness. Thus, if unforgiveness is defined as residual underlying rage at an interpersonal violation, it is easy to see how unforgiveness becomes bad for us. Human beings were not meant to live in a constant state of anger. Whether toxic anger is only the best descriptor of this feeling or is actually the *essence* of unforgiveness must be explored. The problem at hand, however, is that the original offense damages the victim in ways that perpetuate negative feelings.

Level #1: The Sin Itself

Indeed, interpersonal sin causes damage on at least four levels. First there is the original offense and all of its damage, which is significant in itself. Whether the offense consists of an unkind word, a betrayal, an exploitive boundary violation, or a cruel act, sin always takes its toll. Reframing sin into anything less than a moral violation only desensitizes our natural radars and therefore invites a repeat offense.

---

* An often-used synonym for this kind of anger is "resentment," which of course would therefore make resentment an overall bad response. However, I would suggest that Enright's "toxic anger" and Murphy's "resentment" are not the same construct.

Level #2: The Hostile Message of Nonrepentance

In addition to the initial offense, there is the recognition that all actions are also communications. This is the second level of damage. By wronging someone, the offender makes a temporary value judgment about who his victim is and the treatment she deserves. His actions communicate what he thinks. By not repenting, he is solidifying that value judgment in his mind; it is becoming permanent. This posture sends a secondary message to the victim that what the offender did was somehow justified. This message could take many forms, such as, *it was the victim's fault, the offender could not help himself,* or *the victim deserved it.* The exact content of this secondary message may be shaped by circumstances, but all interpersonal sin communicates to the victim the offender's assessment of the victim's value. Furthermore, it communicates that the offender has the power to abuse the victim at will and the victim does not have the power (or moral right) to resist. This message is conveyed in two ways: a) by the offender feeling the freedom to sin against the victim in the first place, and b) by the offender's lack of immediate repentance. Every day that passes without the offender's repentance reinforces the message that the offense was acceptable or justifiable behavior. As long as the offender is working within this mindset (which would be evidence of unrepentance), the victim is faced with the task of processing this hostile message sent by the perpetrator.[5]

Level #3: Self-Inflicted Cognitive Reframes

This leads to a third level of damage heaped upon the victim, but by her own hand. It takes unusual insight to recognize that the message being sent from offender to victim is just that, a message. It is not necessarily the truth; it is just a perspective based upon the offender's behavior. Even if the victim recognizes this behavior as a message rather than as absolute truth, it still takes courage to speak or act upon this knowledge. Most often, the victim does not have the resources to combat these messages and thus begins a process of increasing the harm to herself.

Several destructive responses present themselves to the victim. First, the victim could agree with the offender that the offender's behavior was not morally wrong. Perhaps the offender was acting justly in his treatment of the victim after all, since no one (especially the offender) seems troubled by what happened. Maybe in some way still unclear to the victim, the treatment was deserved. Many sexual abuse victims adopt this position and conclude that it was either their sexual identity itself or their behavior that invited the abuse. Consequently, they initiate a campaign to eradicate uniquely masculine or feminine characteristics so as not to invite a recurrence of the behavior.

While erroneously viewing herself as dangerous to self and others is clearly not healthy, this option at least preserves for the victim the idea that there is some order and logic (and even justice) in the world. One example of a rule learned by experience might go like this: women, even young girls, who allow themselves to be attractive, draw undesired attention from men and invite tragic results. The rule is clear, so now it is just a matter of living in light of it. With these conclusions, it is easy for a victim to shift from a posture of "I hate this about myself" to "I hate myself."[6]

As discouraging as this interpretation ("the offense was justified") might be, it is often the interpretation of choice compared with an even more horrifying explanation—that perhaps there is no such thing as justice after all or a judge who can enforce the law, and the strong can indeed exploit the weak with impunity. In this scenario, no matter what the victim does, she cannot prevent re-abuse. The world is chaotic and evil and those with power can sin unchecked (see the classic books *Animal Farm* and *Lord of the Flies*). Not only is it traumatic to be initially wounded, but it is perhaps even more traumatic to believe that the nature of the world is such that the offender is allowed to escape all consequences. Since this view is oppressive to maintain for any length of time, so many find equilibrium in the first option of justified offense. Others, however, resign themselves to lives of silent despair, while some decide to take their view of justice into their own hands (revenge). Finally, a few conclude that they will no longer live in such a world and take their own lives.

Self-contempt, revenge, and hopelessness are poor choices, but if our internal radar systems have been degraded (as mentioned in Chapter 2), the temptation to distort the truth to regain some equilibrium, however forged, is almost irresistible. The main reason that the victim has to fend off these harmful explanations in the first place is that her offender remains unrepentant, and the message that his behavior was justified remains unchallenged. Even if the victim can somehow hold the dysfunctional interpretations at bay, she still has to face the original harmful message communicated by the offender through his continued unrepentance.

Level #4: Damage to the Relationship

Fourth and finally, absence of repentance creates a rupture in the relationship. It is difficult to trust or be intimate with someone whose behavior warrants resentment (or another term for the same feeling). Legitimate resentment of the offender's behavior therefore presents a logical barrier between victim and offender that inhibits true relationship. In the absence of repentance, the barrier remains and the relationship is strained. Although the victim often feels this pain more acutely and thus is tempted to blame her own bad feelings (resentment) as the main inhibitor to relationship, it is *actually the offender's unrepentance that is the major corrosive agent*. This is why forgiveness ceremonies that do not address these deeper issues are of little help. Is it really forgiveness when each party gives a prepared speech but cannot wait for the performance to conclude so they do not have to interact with each other ever again? Whatever else may be gained by such a dialogue, it is not forgiveness.

Sadly, loss of relationship is the logical final result of a cascade of damage beginning with an offense, the message behind the offense, and the dysfunctional interpretations added by the victim. These are just a few of the reasons why the feelings resulting from interpersonal sin are so uncomfortable, and may explain why forgiveness writers are so eager to reduce these feelings by explaining them away and prematurely encouraging victims to release them without full recognition of their effects.

In light of this chain reaction of damage beginning with a moral offense, is it possible for anyone to mentally recognize this process without having *some* emotional reaction? Do we not feel grief for the victim when we understand that she will be tempted to explain her world in a twisted fashion and that this temptation might haunt her for the rest of her life? Even in cases where victims can correctly identify moral violations and challenge the harmful underlying messages that emerge from them, there remains a sense of injustice that the victim must heal from a wound inflicted upon her through no fault of her own. Would we not expect the victim to be somewhat irritated (or dismayed or at least some other negative feeling) at the extra work (i.e., counseling, support groups, etc.) now required of her just to remain healthy?*

---

* This is why trauma does such long-standing damage because it requires a self-perpetuating cycle of "therapy" that implies that the victim is not well.

What about the offender? Do we not feel some kind of anger that he would wound another human being in the first place, and even more anger when he refuses to take responsibility for or even acknowledge what he has done? If the victim has come to a place where she can correctly identify the original offense as a true moral violation, would she not then also experience some kind of unpleasant response when the offender continues to communicate an alternative and degrading message? She could legitimately respond with something like, "What you did was wrong and I resent the fact that you still think it was acceptable. And I really resent that I have to remind myself of these truths regularly because your actions have energized strong self-blaming and self-contemptuous temptations in me that now I have to ward off. And finally, I resent that your behavior has poisoned and maybe ended our relationship." Is there anything toxic or ulcer-inducing in these sentiments, or do they reflect a fully *appropriate* response to the mistreatment of one created in the image of God? I would suggest that to *deny* the resentment in this case would be more unhealthy and unworthy of Him whose image we bear.

AFFECTIVE RESPONSE TO SIN

It should not surprise us that those created in the image of God not only recognize sin cognitively but also respond affectively. God Himself responds to sin both cognitively and affectively, that is, He allows Himself to respond *emotionally* to sin. While the term "wrath of God" admittedly has theological (John 3:36; Eph. 2:3) and eschatological (Rev. 6:17) connotations, the fact that a term like "wrath" is used in the first place indicates that God is a god of very strong feelings. God really is angry at sin and the Bible describes God's anger as burning (Isa. 30:27) and constant (it is expressed every day, according to Psalm 7:11). Not only are God's feelings about sin intense, but they are also responsive. When God *heard* His people complaining about their lack of meat (in reality, a criticism of His goodness), He *reacted* by getting very angry (Ps. 78:21). Jesus also *responded* with anger when He saw the hardness of heart reflected in His critics' faces (Mark 3:5). Finally, Jesus became so enraged when He *saw* His Father's house becoming a place of economic exploitation rather than a house of prayer, that His disciples were reminded of the psalmist's statement, "zeal for Your house will consume me" (John 2:17; cf. Ps. 69:9). These are just a few examples of God's strong *emotional* response to sin.

51

There are those who would emphasize the profound distinction between God's anger, usually referred to as righteous indignation, and human anger, which is usually little more than an outgrowth of selfish petulance. This is a legitimate caution and since the fall of humanity, most human anger is tainted with something more than just passion for God and His reputation. However, if all human anger is discounted as sinful, then humans are left with little more than a cognitive capacity to recognize evil, without any emotional motivation to do anything about it.

Indeed, something in the heart of a believer should be emotionally repulsed by sin. Jonathan Edwards, the well-known eighteenth-century American Puritan, claimed that humans never behold anything as indifferent, unaffected spectators, but instead are always either *inclined toward* something or *inclined away* from it. He wrote, "In every act of the will whatsoever, the soul either likes or dislikes, is either inclined or disinclined to what is in view: these are not *essentially* different from the affections of *love* and *hatred*."[7] If we respond to everything with either love or hate (regardless of how minimal) then maybe some of our outrage at sin is normal.

Scripture also supports this idea that a cognitive appraisal of evil will always be accompanied by some affective response. For example, the psalmist requires those that *love* God to *hate* evil (Ps. 97:10). True love does not merely recognize truth but *rejoices* in it (1 Cor. 13:6). Conversely, Paul commands his readers to not only correctly identify that which is evil but also to *abhor* it (Rom. 12:9). Again, no one can serve two masters, in that it is impossible not to be affectively drawn more toward one than toward the other.

Another concern with this reconstructed and more positive view of resentment is that it could be perceived as a cover for revenge. However, a longing for justice is not the same as appointing oneself as judge. Revenge only demonstrates that the victim now has power to inflict damage on the perpetrator, but it does not validate the victim in any way. In fact, it lowers the victim to the level of the offender. Revenge, often touted as a "dish best served cold," still leaves a sour taste in our mouths. This is why victims do not ultimately want revenge; they want justice. The longing is for some judge *above both* victim and offender to take the victim's side and enforce justice. A victim wants to be validated; destroying an unrepentant sinner does not accomplish this.

If all of this is true, then some of the strong feelings experienced as a result of interpersonal sin may actually be *healthy*. Could these uncomfortable emotional reactions hitherto labeled as toxic resentment actually emerge from the tension of a *legitimate* longing for justice in a world that is so unfair? And if so, could there be an appropriate time to be angry? If Murphy, who does not write from a distinctively Christian perspective, makes a case for legitimate resentment based on a love of justice,[8] how much more should the child of God, who knows and loves the God of all justice, be offended when injustice appears to hold sway so often? If we pray "Thy kingdom come," are we not praying for a world where justice will "roll down like waters and righteousness like an ever-flowing stream" (Amos 5:24), and would this not, by necessity, include God's judgment for sin?

As they pray for God's kingdom to come, His people are often tempted to wonder if justice will ever be done. For one who believes in a sovereign, holy, and loving God, this can be a real test of faith. At times the child of God has to make sense of the fact that her heavenly Father allowed something to occur that was clearly unjust. Despite claims to the contrary (2 Chron. 19:7), the victim could begin to wonder if God has indeed been "bought off," and she could be tempted to conclude with the psalmist that God has "sold her cheaply" (see Ps. 44:12).

Justice, then, is the crux of the matter. Interpersonal sin is an assault on justice and the God of justice. Feelings of resentment or legitimate anger are both a *logical* and *appropriate* response to injustice. Resentment is logical if it is defined as merely an emotional reaction to what has already been recognized cognitively—that is, that an offense has been committed and the offender is not repentant. Resentment defined this way is also appropriate because God Himself reacts to sin with such strong, affectively laden, negative feelings.

Even if these feelings of resentment are more valid than previously thought, they are still not pleasant. Resentment, to whatever degree legitimate, still does not feel very good and that often can become the primary motive for getting rid of it. Whether it is morally defensible or not, who wants to endure a cloud of painful emotions for an indeterminate time period? Yet, in a sinful world, all creation continually groans as a result of the futility and corruption rampant since the fall. Moreover, even those with the firstfruits of the Spirit still groan waiting for the day when all will be made right and they will be clothed with their dwelling from heaven (Rom. 8:20–23; 2 Cor. 5:2). If some kind of groaning is actually normative for the Christian life, we must be careful not to judge our feelings simply by their level of pleasantness. Many times painful feelings are sinful, but not always. Sometimes they are normal responses and therefore we should not be so quick to dismiss them.

Here psychology and counseling can sometimes be a hindrance rather than a help, for the people-helping field (including Christian counselors) often confuses the uncomfortable *feelings* resulting from the problem with the problem itself. The real problem, the offender's continued unrepentance, is out of everyone's control except the offender's. Rather than risk being immobilized by grief and despair, the modified goal then becomes something more empowering, to either neutralize or deconstruct the negative feelings so they will go away. If I can somehow help my clients feel better (or at least not feel so bad) I must be helping them to get healthy.

The problem with this approach is that feelings can be dealt with apart from the real problems ever being addressed. If feelings are the real problem, there are many ways to reduce any negative feelings apart from dealing with the real issue. Some just get tired of resenting and experience some kind of memory fatigue as a result. After a while, it becomes exhausting to continue feeling bad, especially if the offense was long ago.

However, many are unable to banish the memory and the related feelings to remote memory cells. In such cases there are many ways to, in effect, deny them on a regular basis. First is *passive denial*. This is just a simple, deliberate choice not to think about the painful memories. If that does not work, there is always the strategy of thinking differently about what happened. This could be called *denial by subterfuge* or in clinical terms, a *cognitive reframe* as mentioned earlier with all of its pernicious repercussions. If a victim can reconstruct her memories or interpretations of events, she can significantly alter the negative feelings that emerge from them. Finally, there is denial in the name of God, or *pious denial*.[9] The victim can pray, memorize Scripture, or practice other spiritual disciplines to devoutly outdistance the intensity of the memories or the pain of the offender's continued unrepentance.

But if the feelings are a result of damage, then it is the damage that needs to be addressed rather than just the feelings that emerge from the damage. Healing from the damage will go a long way toward reducing feelings that are ultimately harmful. Yet apart from the offender's repentance, some painful feelings will still remain, whether these feelings are identified as resentment, grief, or something else. Imagine the range of emotions in the father's quiet moments as he reflected on the behavior of his prodigal son. As he prayed for his son to return, it is hard to imagine the absence of at least some unpleasant feelings. These feelings must be embraced without succumbing to the temptation to misuse them on the one hand or to pretend they do not exist on the other.

How does this discussion relate to forgiveness? As noted, God has infinite reason to feel resentment and yet He does not sin. The resentment that God feels does not lead to any further damage to Him, nor does it overwhelm His character or become addictive. In spite of all of the rebellious secondary and tertiary messages we send to God by our behavior, He resists the temptation to sin in response. Furthermore, He stands ready to forgive. Although God resents sin more than any human does, He remains the chief forgiver in Scripture and provides the template for how we can forgive. It is incumbent upon us, then, to understand the manner in which God forgives.

MODELING GOD'S FORGIVENESS

. . . forgiving each other, just as God **in Christ** *has also forgiven you.*

—Ephesians 4:32 (emphasis added)

Just as the Lord forgave you, so also *should you.*

—Colossians 3:13 (emphasis added)

C hapter 1 listed four characteristics of forgiveness according to Scripture. First, forgiveness is based on divine forgiveness, not human projections. Second, it presupposes rather than causes healing. Third, it is active rather than passive; and finally, it is other-centered as opposed to self-centered. These characteristics are intertwined, for I believe that God's method of forgiveness will exhibit an active, other-centered focus from a position of health. As we seek to model Christ in our forgiveness, we should also exhibit these three other characteristics. The first task, then, is to determine how it is that God forgives.

In the biblical narrative describing forgiveness, God is clearly the main character. His forgiveness of wayward human beings constitutes the majority of the forgiveness texts (i.e., Exod. 34:7; Ps. 51; 86:5; 1 John 1:9). Even in the few passages that refer specifically to human interpersonal forgiveness, there is often a link to divine forgiveness either directly or indirectly (e.g., "Forgive us us our debts, as we also have forgiven our debtors," Matt. 6:12). If God is the ultimate model, it is of utmost importance to determine what really happens when God forgives someone.

There are seven words in the Bible that are translated *forgive*, as well as several related terms and phrases that incorporate the ideas of forgiveness.* The two most common terms (one Old Testament and one New Testament) allude to the cancelling of a debt. The other words have slightly different emphases, but every term for forgiveness incorporates a forensic or economic sense of a debt being cancelled. However, these words defined in a vacuum describe only a small piece of the overall concept of forgiveness. Word studies alone fail to answer key complex questions: What is the debt that needs to be cancelled? Under what conditions is it cancelled? Is the offender at all involved, or can the debt be cancelled unilaterally? For a precise description of what actually transpires during the act of forgiveness and under what conditions it occurs, the context must be considered.

The presentation of God's forgiveness as a model for human interpersonal forgiveness is stated most clearly in two key biblical texts where these concepts are linked:

> So, as those who have been chosen by God, holy and beloved, put on a heart of compassion, kindness, humility, gentleness and patience; bearing with one another, and forgiving one another, whoever has a complaint against anyone: *just as the Lord forgave you, so also* should you (Col. 3:12–13, emphasis added).

> Let all bitterness and wrath and anger and clamor and slander be put away from you, along with all malice. Be kind to one another, tender-hearted, forgiving each other just as God *in Christ* also has forgiven you (Eph. 4:31–32, emphasis added).

Both of these passages list interpersonal forgiveness as one of many virtues that emerge in one who has been raised with Christ (Col. 3:1) or has put on the new self (Eph. 4:24). Thus, whatever forgiveness

---

* For a list of the various words in the original languages used for forgiveness in the Bible, see the *International Standard Bible Encyclopedia* or one of many Bible word-study books.

might mean, it is clear from these texts that it occurs along with the divine renewal of the heart. This shapes the fact that though the word for forgiveness in both texts is an imperative,* it should not be overemphasized to the exclusion of the conditions and stipulations under which forgiveness is to be granted. In the Colossians text for example, it must be noted that this command is a result of the conclusion drawn in 3:1 that introduces the whole passage. The capacity to forgive as this text directs rests not only on following God's model but also in trusting in His power to change lives based on the fact that the readers have been raised with Christ. Since these two passages link interpersonal forgiveness with divine forgiveness, a closer examination of the wording is in order.

KEY TERMS

Forgive

The word for forgiveness is the same word used in both texts. It is the second most common term used in the New Testament for forgiveness and literally means "to lavishly grace one another."[1] Or put another way, "freely give to one another." Although Paul uses both terms for forgiveness, the second term is exclusive to him. Paul often uses both terms in the same forensic or economic sense, such as earlier in Colossians 1:14 where he uses the most common word and Colossians 2:23 where he uses the second most common word. By the time of the Pauline epistles, it appears that the words have become almost synonymous, at least in how Paul uses them. Whatever the semantic possibilities, the final conceptualization of forgiveness in these texts is governed by the qualifier "*just as* the Lord forgave you."

Just As

The conjunction "just as" is only one word in the original and usually links two objects or concepts being compared. It could be translated "in like manner" and it is used this way throughout Colossians. Paul first uses it in his greeting, when he states that he is thankful for the gospel that had reached the Colossians *in like manner* as it was

---

* Both times, the word for "forgive" is actually a participle but is used as an imperative.

permeating the known world (1:6). The way that the gospel came to them was similar to the way the gospel had arrived in other parts of the world. Contrary to some of the theological and philosophical errors that were tempting the Colossian believers, the gospel was being proclaimed to all; it was not the privileged domain of Jewish legalists, Greek philosophers, or Eastern mystics.

Paul is pleased that this gospel that had spread throughout the world was bearing fruit *in like manner* as it was in the lives of the Colossian saints. Colossians 1:6 could be worded this way, "I am thankful that the gospel has reached you *in like manner* as it has reached the whole world. Furthermore, the gospel is bearing fruit throughout the world *in like manner* as it is in you." In addition, this gospel that was spreading and having such an impact was not just any gospel; it was the "word of truth" (v. 5). This was the same gospel ("just as") that the Colossians had learned from Paul's fellow bondservant Epaphras, whom Paul identified as a "faithful servant of Christ on our behalf" (v. 7). To summarize, Paul was thankful that the gospel received by the Colossian believers was the same dynamic gospel being preached throughout the world *and* was the same gospel they had learned from Epaphras.

Another time "just as" is used this way is in Colossians 2:7, where Paul links "being firmly rooted and built up in Him" *in like manner* as the previous instruction the Colossians had received. They were not to go looking for new and creative ways to know God better (like legalism or mysticism), but rather were to look to what they had been originally taught by Paul and others for guidance and growth.

This extended treatment of the phrase "just as" helps to clarify what the apostle is actually calling for as it relates to forgiveness in 3:13. The reader is not at liberty to project any meaning onto forgiveness; rather, the forgiveness called for is modeled after (*in like manner*) God's forgiveness—*as God forgave you*. Some might take this phrase as merely indicating precedent and translate the phrase as "because." In other words, in this passage, believers are to forgive primarily *because* God forgave them, not necessarily *in the same way*. This type of statement, however, usually uses a different word structure. In addition, the fact that "just as" is used in a comparative sense several times in Colossians makes this usage more likely. As if this were not enough, Paul adds the phrase "*so also* should you," which only strengthens the comparative sense of the word.

In Christ

In the Ephesians passage, a modifying condition is added to the directive to forgive in like manner as God. The forgiveness Paul is calling his readers to practice is not only *in like manner* as God forgave them, but is also "in Christ" or "for Christ's sake." What does this mean? The command to "lavishly grace one another" must be based on Christ and His work; otherwise, why add this stipulation? Forgiveness must somehow always be linked to the gospel. Any definition of forgiveness that is not rooted in the gospel drifts from the biblical concept of forgiveness.

Examining the full meaning of the gospel would take many books but here the role of the gospel in forgiveness must be clarified. The gospel (and the forgiveness available through it) is firmly rooted in the sacrificial death and triumphant resurrection of Jesus (1 Cor. 15:3–4). Indeed, without Christ's substitutionary atonement, there could be no forgiveness (Heb. 9:22). God's holiness cannot be compromised by sin, so Christ took the penalty for humanity's rebellion through His death on the cross. His ultimate victory was demonstrated by His resurrection from the dead, but this too looks back to the cross as the means of finally defeating evil. Apart from the death and resurrection of Jesus, there is no gospel. Without the gospel, there is no forgiveness, and then our faith is worthless, because we are still in our sins and are to be understandably pitied (1 Cor. 15:14–19). On the other hand, because of Christ's atonement, forgiveness is available from God and subsequently from one another.

These two "forgive one another" passages establish two key characteristics of divine forgiveness. First, God has a manner in which He forgives; and second, God's manner of forgiving is firmly rooted in the gospel. Since we are instructed to model our forgiveness after God's example, we too must base our forgiveness on the gospel, which itself reveals at least four characteristics about God's forgiveness.

FOUR CHARACTERISTICS OF GOD'S FORGIVENESS

God's Forgiveness Comes Naturally

Unlike humans, God is predisposed to forgive ("For You, Lord, are good, and ready to forgive," Ps. 86:5). Like His amazing love, forgiveness is simply a part of His nature ("To the Lord our God belong compassion and forgiveness," Dan. 9:9). He does not have to be bribed or talked into it. God does not forgive to lower His blood pressure or to sleep better at night. He does not forgive to rid Himself of toxic anger, for all of His anger is a fully appropriate and righteous response by a holy God to sin. So why does God even want to forgive? The simple and yet profound answer is that God longs to forgive because that is just the way He is. He is always ready to forgive and nothing slows Him down, because He is always love.

None of us is God and because of our sinful nature, we do not naturally gravitate toward extending forgiveness. Part of becoming more like Christ, however, is acquiring a desire for forgiveness and reconciliation whenever possible. But this desire is often overwhelmed by a desire for revenge that energizes a momentum away from forgiveness rather than toward it.

God's Forgiveness Is Other-Centered

Our loving God focuses on us; He is other-centered. This is the second characteristic of His forgiveness. God actively pursues sinners in order to forgive them for *their* benefit. God does not conduct a unilateral forgiveness ceremony so He can let go of the pain. He does not forgive alone, nor does He forgive to make Himself feel better or heal from the wounds we have inflicted upon Him. He forgives sinners face to face in response to repentance and faith. Those forgiven are described as blessed or happy ("How blessed is he whose transgression is forgiven," Ps. 32:1), and pardon for sin is the first benefit listed in Psalm 103 for those who bless God's name. When God forgives, sinners are not only personally involved in the process but are radically changed *through* the process.

If we are to imitate God, our forgiveness, though it may result in various health benefits to us, should not be done for those reasons. Just like God, our forgiveness also needs to be other-centered. This seriously calls into question the idea that we can forgive apart from any involvement with the offender. How can our forgiveness be other-centered when it is something we do primarily by and for ourselves? Naturally, if the offender is dead, there must be some kind of closure for the victim. But is this *forgiveness*? Those who die unrepentant are not afforded God's forgiveness. If God Himself does not grant forgiveness to the unrepentant, would He expect their victims to do otherwise?

This also calls into question the idea of forgiving ourselves. Of course, because He is perfect, God never has an occasion to forgive Himself. Beyond that, it is difficult to imagine one part of our self confessing sin to another part that is in a position to absolve it. In addition, there is the thoroughly confusing issue of *how* or even *should* we forgive ourselves? Is there a formal apology in front of a mirror? How about a note from one self to another self? And how do we know we have sufficiently and completely forgiven ourselves? Is there any part of our selves (the plural here is deliberate) that can be trusted to forgive the other parts of ourselves? How can we be sure that we will not be too hard (or soft) on ourselves?

These questions expose the logical problems with the entire concept of forgiving ourselves. Perhaps the greatest fallacy with this view is that for every offense, there is always more than one victim. David sinned against several people in his adultery with Bathsheba but it was his offense *against God* that anguished him most, as he lamented, "Against You, You only, I have sinned and done what is evil in Your sight" (Ps. 51:4). If a moral violation occurs, our greatest concern should not be whether we can forgive ourselves but rather whether God will forgive us. If God pronounces us forgiven, what right do we have to resurrect the charges?*

God's Forgiveness Is Rooted in the Substitutionary Atonement

What motivates God to forgive is His love; what *allows* Him to forgive is Christ's work on the cross. This is the third characteristic of God's forgiveness: it is based on the substitutionary atonement of Christ. Indeed, sacrifice for sin, forgiveness, and grace are frequently linked throughout Scripture, as in Ephesians: "In Him we have redemption *through His blood, the forgiveness of our trespasses*, according to the riches of His *grace*" (Eph. 1:7, emphasis added); and Romans: "being justified as a gift by His *grace* through the redemption which is in Christ Jesus; whom God displayed publicly as a propitiation *in His blood* through faith" (Rom. 3:24–25).

---

* I realize that there is probably a lot more going on in the hearts of those who claim to struggle with forgiving themselves. It can be a cover-up for the shock and grief of having to face that they were capable of more evil than they thought, or it can be an excuse to remain self-focused in response to God's call to other-centered love. Whatever the case, my only point here is that "forgiveness" is not the correct term for this concept.

Because redemption from sin is the basis for God's forgiveness, He has no need to muster up feelings of empathy to help reduce His resentment. He already knows why we sin ("The heart is more deceitful. . . . Who can understand it? I, the Lord, search the heart," Jer. 17:9–10). That is part of the problem. Our sin is not an accident or a careless blunder; it is utter rebellion. Thus God has no need to view things from our perspective (although He can); we need to see things from *His* perspective. Empathizing with our rebellion would not change the fact that we are guilty, nor would it facilitate any kind of reconciliation. To be reconciled to God requires a price to be paid. This is why the forensic view of forgiveness (to use the language of Chapter 1) must be primary. Without the price for sin being paid, there can be no forgiveness, relational or otherwise.

God's Forgiveness Requires Repentance

The final characteristic of God's forgiveness is that it requires repentance on the part of the offender. Because addressing sin is the prerequisite for reconciling with God, confession and repentance* must be part of the process. First John 1:9 identifies confession (literally "to say the same thing as") as a prerequisite to forgiveness. Furthermore, if we try to deny our sin we not only call God a deceiver, but expose ourselves as victims of our own self-deception (1 John 1:8, 10).

The view that repentance is required for forgiveness is admittedly not the majority position of most forgiveness writers. As mentioned earlier, from a purely psychological viewpoint, the "repentance not required" view has its advantages in that the offender cannot disrupt or interfere with the process. Nothing supposedly stands in the way of the victim performing some kind of cognitive reframe and moving on with her life. This change of attitude, though unilateral in nature, could be viewed as at least indirectly beneficial to the offender in that the victim no longer views the offender with hostility.

From a Christian perspective, however, the key question is whether the Bible supports forgiveness apart from repentance and confession. Can someone release resentment toward her offender in some private ceremony

---

*   I recognize that these two words carry different connotations but for the purpose of this study I will be using them interchangeably under the assumption that anyone who truly agrees with God about the true nature of their sin will subsequently want to turn around and repent.

before God and then count that as forgiveness? On the other hand, if repentance is required, then when faced with the absence of repentance, can forgiveness actually be postponed (without all of the negative side effects)? As is the case with many scriptural questions, there are texts that appear to support both sides, and each side is saddled with the task of somehow defending against the proof texts of the other. On the issue of whether repentance is required for forgiveness, there are several texts that clearly make forgiveness contingent upon the offender's response.

In the two primary passages detailing how interpersonal sin should be handled in the church, repentance is presented as the key prerequisite to forgiveness. After confronting the offender, "*if he listens to you*, you have won your brother" (Matt. 18:15, emphasis added); and "*if he repents*, forgive him" (Luke 17:3, emphasis added). Even in the case where it might appear that the repentance is lacking in sincerity (repeat offending seven times in the same day!) repentance is still required in order for forgiveness to be granted (Luke 17:4).

Luke's version of the Great Commission states that "repentance for forgiveness of sins would be proclaimed in His name to all the nations" (24:47). The disciples took this mandate seriously, as evidenced by Peter's invitation to the crowd to "repent . . . for the forgiveness of your sins" following his convicting sermon during Pentecost (Acts 2:38). In his next sermon shortly thereafter, he again exhorted his hearers, "repent . . . so that your sins may be wiped away" (Acts 3:19). Even when he was called to defend his actions before the high priest, Peter maintained that his message was to preach Christ as Savior, who could "grant repentance to Israel and forgiveness of sins" (Acts 5:31). Years later when Paul had his turn to defend his message, he too proclaimed that the goal of the gospel was "to open their eyes so they may turn from darkness to light . . . that they may receive forgiveness of sins" (Acts 26:18). Finally, the apostle John, hearkening back to Psalm 32:5, links confession with forgiveness in his famous forgiveness formula: "If we confess our sins, He is faithful and righteous to forgive us our sins and to cleanse us from all unrighteousness" (1 John 1:9).

These are the main passages that support the view that forgiveness is contingent upon repentance. However, there are many passages where no contingencies are listed for forgiveness (Acts 10:43), including the two key passages on interpersonal forgiveness (Eph. 4:32; Col. 3:13) examined at the beginning of this chapter. The strongest passages supporting this view are the stories of Jesus from the cross, praying that God would apparently forgive unilaterally and unconditionally (Luke 23:34). Likewise, Stephen does not add any conditions when he prays to God, "do not hold this sin against them" (Acts 7:60).

So which set of passages are the most persuasive? Is repentance required for forgiveness or not? There seem to be only three ways to harmonize these passages: 1) repentance is required for forgiveness; 2) repentance is not required for forgiveness; or 3) a compromise position. Those taking the view that repentance is indeed required would refer to the passages in which this is taught as normative. Once it is understood that repentance is required, it becomes an unspoken assumption even in passages where it is not mentioned.

Those who maintain that repentance is not required for forgiveness must come up with some kind of hierarchy of forgiveness to explain the passages where repentance seems to be required. Perhaps forgiveness at its most basic level (unilateral and unconditional) would not require anything on the part of the offender and it is this kind of forgiveness spoken of in the many passages that do not mention repentance. However, if or when repentance does finally happen, there might be a deeper level of forgiveness that can occur involving a true relational improvement between the offender and the offended. For this relational rupture to be healed, repentance must be part of the process. This explains the texts that make forgiveness contingent upon repentance.

The compromise position would be to claim that in certain situations repentance is required and in others it is not. While this appears to resolve the tension initially, the task of identifying which situations or sins warrant repentance and which do not could create many more problems than it solves. Who decides? Is forgiveness in response to repentance the same as that granted apart from repentance?

While each position has it strengths, I hold to the first view because I think it is the strongest from a biblical perspective. I believe repentance is required for forgiveness and once this is a given, it does not have to be mentioned in every text to reaffirm or prove it. Of course anyone who holds this position has to answer for Jesus's words on the cross: "Father, forgive them, for they know not what they are doing"—a clear example of forgiveness without any evidence of repentance by anyone (except eventually one of the thieves crucified with Christ).

D. A. Carson has advised that this passage be considered carefully before being used to prove anything. He gives four considerations that must be kept in mind when attempting to use this text to normalize any view of forgiveness.[2] First, when Christ says that the reason forgiveness should be granted is because "they know not what they are doing," this cannot mean total ignorance; otherwise, there would be nothing to forgive. The people may have been ignorant of whom they were crucifying, but even Pilate recognized that they were putting to death an innocent man. Even if ignorance becomes the condition whereby repentance is no longer required, this only applies to cases in which the offender is truly lacking in understanding, which are probably only a minority of cases.

Carson's second point is that it is not clear who the object is of Christ's request that they be forgiven. Was it those clustered around the base of the cross—the Jewish scorners, and the Romans gambling for his garments? Maybe it was the Jewish nation or the Romans or maybe humanity in general. Without a clear-cut identification of whom Christ was pleading for, it is difficult to use this passage as a standard for forgiveness.

Third, it is not clear how or even when Christ's prayer was answered. Did God grant blanket forgiveness for everyone for everything that day? Or is Christ's prayer for forgiveness still being answered even today as people recognize why Christ was really being crucified and accept Him as Savior? Finally, Carson suggests that perhaps these words from the cross were meant to provide a window into Christ's heart rather than to make a normative statement on forgiveness.

So what did Christ mean when He asked His heavenly Father to forgive those who were ignorant of what they were doing? Again, it must be determined as to what they were ignorant. A clue comes from a similar statement by Stephen as he was being martyred. While he was dying, he prayed, "Lord, do not hold *this sin* against them!" (Acts 7:60, emphasis added). It seems that Stephen was asking that the sin of killing one of God's messengers not be put to their account. Did they know what they were doing? Apparently there was some ignorance on the part of Saul/Paul, as he believed passionately that he was persecuting the church to glorify God; and yet on the way to Damascus shortly thereafter, he came to see that he had actually been waging war with the God he thought he was serving (Acts 9). Similar to Stephen, Christ could be asking that those responsible for killing the Son of God be forgiven for this one particular offense. Some sins may have no remedy except by arbitrary, unilateral forgiveness by the Son of God. Whatever forgiveness means in these passages, it should not serve as the normative framework for whether repentance is required or not. These passages do not therefore diminish the argument for repentance being required.

Thus, forgiveness, as it was intended to work, must involve repentance on the part of the offender. Without this repentance, forgiveness can and in some cases *must be* postponed. The idea of postponing forgiveness may seem difficult to justify, but what if the appropriate conditions for forgiveness have more to do with the offender's response than the victim's? The current thought seems to lean more heavily toward whether the victim will *choose* to forgive rather than whether the offender will *choose* to repent. What if sin *cannot* be truly forgiven apart from repentance? Martin Luther actually seems to be saying this in his comments on Matthew 18:18:

> There are two kinds of sin: one kind is confessed, and this no one should leave unforgiven; the other kind is defended, and this *no one can forgive*, for it refuses either to be counted as sin or to accept forgiveness. It is *impossible* to loose a sin which a person refuses to acknowledge as a sin that needs to be forgiven; such a sin should be bound to the abyss of hell.[3]

Even God cannot arbitrarily forgive apart from a turning around on the part of the offender. Indeed, when Jesus looked over the city of Jerusalem, He lamented that although He greatly desired to restore the city, their continual rejection of Him actually prevented Him (Matt. 23:37).

If God must postpone forgiveness due to unrepentance, humans also are restricted in their forgiveness of one another. Just like God, we should always be ready to forgive, but until the conditions are met, forgiveness cannot be granted. In this extended quote, Luther applies what he said earlier to interpersonal sin. If Luther is correct, *every* sin that is not repented of becomes an unpardonable sin.

> This provision in the office of the keys also applies to the relation of every Christian with his neighbor. He should be *ready* to

forgive everyone that injures him. And yet, if someone refuses to acknowledge the sin and to stop it, but persists in it, you *cannot* forgive him—not on your account but on his, because he refuses to accept the forgiveness. But as soon as he owns up to being guilty and requests forgiveness, everything must be granted, and the absolution must follow right away. Since he is punishing himself and desisting from his sin, so that there is no longer any sin about him, I should let the matter of his sin drop. But if he holds on to it and refuses to drop it, I *cannot* take it from him but must let him remain stuck in it; for *he himself* has changed a *forgivable* sin into an *unforgivable* one. In other words if he refuses to confess, his conscience must be burdened as heavily as possible, without any sign of grace; for he stubbornly insists upon being the devil's own. On the other hand, if he confesses his sin and begs your pardon but you refuse to forgive him, you have loaded the sin upon yourself, and it will condemn you as well.[4]

There are two other passages linking divine and human forgiveness that warrant at least brief comments. First, in the parable of the two debtors (Matt. 18:21–35), one servant owes his lord an amount that is impossible to pay back. He begs to be given the chance to pay it off but instead the lord in the story cancels the entire debt. Shortly after, the same servant refuses to forgive a coworker who owed him a very manageable amount. When the lord finds out, he has the first man jailed. The lesson according to Jesus is, "My heavenly Father will also do the same to you, if each of you does not forgive his brother from your heart" (v. 35).* The whole parable was given in response to Peter's question about how many times a repentant brother should be forgiven (v. 21). The answer from the story is that just as our Lord (to whom we owe more than we could ever pay) is always compassionate and ready to forgive those who recognize their debt, so we should be ever prepared to forgive all those who repent for what they have done to us, no matter how many times it takes.

---

*   It is interesting that the phrase "from the heart" is added. Does this imply that there is an outer superficial form of forgiveness that does not really interest God? See Chapter 5 for Spring's construct of cheap forgiveness.

The forgiveness asked for in the Lord's Prayer is similar (Matt. 6:9–13). As mentioned earlier, repentance is not mentioned as a prerequisite to forgiveness in this text. It does not have to be, since it can be implied from other passages. The point of the Lord's Prayer is that we cannot choose the unconditional unrepentance option (Spring's Option 1, discussed in Chapter 5) if we are truly children of God. As the Lord has forgiven us (in response to confession and repentance), so we should be ready and willing to forgive those who repent. In both of these passages a large part of the motive for forgiving others is that we ourselves have been forgiven, for a lot! However, regardless of how much we owe, God has forgiven us. So we should forgive others. Thus, God's manner of forgiveness, as we are able to describe it from Scripture, includes: a readiness to forgive, an other-centered focus, a foundation in the gospel, and a requirement of repentance.

CHAPTER 5

THE GOD WHO KEEPS SCORE

O Lord, God of vengeance, God of vengeance, shine forth!
—Psalm 94:1

The first characteristic of biblical forgiveness is that it is modeled after God's forgiveness. As mentioned in the previous chapter, God does not forgive so that He can heal from anything. While our sin does hurt Him, it does not trigger any sinful cognitive or behavioral responses. He is fully intact and healthy (if such words can be applied to God) and can thus pursue His wayward people from a position of strength and true love. He does not *need* us to repent in order to process His pain. Therefore, the forgiveness that He offers is for *our* benefit, not His.

One implication of this view of God's forgiveness is that repentance, while required for forgiveness, is *not* required for healing. Second, healing (but perhaps not forgiveness) can be achieved apart from any action by the offender. It could be said that healing is about how we respond to the offense, while forgiveness is about how we respond to the offender (when a response is warranted). It is important at this stage to differentiate healing and forgiveness. Healing can be characterized as unilateral, self-focused, and laying the groundwork for forgiveness. Forgiveness, on the other hand, must be bilateral, other-focused, and occur as a result of healing.

For many forgiveness writers, these distinctions are blurred or non-existent. Either healing comes *through* forgiveness (either bilateral or unilateral), or healing is just another term for forgiveness. It gets even more confusing when forgiveness is disconnected from any relational change. In this case forgiveness is usually unilateral. The idea is that a victim can forgive in a unilateral fashion without anything from the offender. In contrast, restoring the relationship *does* depend on the offender and his willingness to repent and change. This distinction allows the victim to claim she is following the mandate to forgive, but it really does not change anything outside of her own mind. It also can lead the victim to conclude that the forgiveness process can actually be complete apart from any action whatsoever by the offender. If forgiveness is offered unilaterally and prior to the offender's repentance, what is there left to offer if and when the offender eventually does repent? According to the unilateral view, forgiveness is already complete and has nothing to do with restoration of the relationship. All the victim could say is, "I already forgave you; I don't know what I can do for you now."

So how do we heal from interpersonal sin and thus begin to prepare for forgiveness? Janis Abrahms Spring recognizes the tension inherent in the usual forgiveness taxonomy, and presents three common responses to interpersonal violations and one alternative response, although all have drawbacks. The first is blatantly unhealthy, the second depends on the actions of someone else, and the third (and most common) response is superficial and does not really accomplish anything.[1] Each of these options, including her viable alternative, warrants further examination.

Spring's Responses to Interpersonal Violations

Option 1: Refusal to Forgive

The first potential response to interpersonal sin is an absolute refusal to forgive under any conditions. This is typically a self-protective posture based on the cynical beliefs that people rarely change their behavior, and that confession and apologies are little more than manipulative stunts or power plays. No matter what the offender says or does, the victim chooses safety rather than relationship. This could be called unconditional unforgiveness. Spring warns that this option hinders relationships and promotes loneliness. A biblical example is that of Jonah, who through his unforgiving posture eventually valued shade-producing plants over people. There are too many passages in Scripture calling for forgiveness to allow a Christian to take this option.

Option 2: Genuine Forgiveness

Real or genuine forgiveness is the preferred option for Spring. However, this option is not always available. Three characteristics make this forgiveness authentic and all three of these conditions must be met or the forgiveness is not genuine. First, true forgiveness is transactional; that is, it represents an exchange *between two people*. Offender and offended are in dialogue and each provides a necessary component to the discussion. Thus, this type of forgiveness cannot be unilateral.

The second characteristic of this type of forgiveness is that it is conditional. In Spring's model, the condition consists of the stated desire and subsequent behavior of the offender. The offender must agree that what he did was wrong, express regret, and do whatever it takes to make it right. Thus, according to Spring, forgiveness must be earned through the gradual process of restoring trust by means of such atoning behavior.

Repentance is the closest biblical term for this process, although there is no stated justification in Scripture for postponing forgiveness until the offered repentance proves sufficient enough to earn forgiveness. True confession (indicative of repentance) is the only requirement and the forgiveness is given immediately, even to the tune of seven times a day (Luke 17:4). Evaluating the level and quality of someone's repentance is always a judgment call, but at the end of the day we are to trust that the turnaround we are seeing is real.

Spring's final characteristic of genuine forgiveness is that it involves a transfer of vigilance. After forgiveness has been granted, it is no longer the victim's responsibility to make sure forgiveness has been done correctly or even done at all. It is up to the offender to demonstrate that forgiveness has really been granted by his change in behavior.

While this transfer of vigilance is not expressly mentioned in Scripture, there are several examples in which those called on to repent are also called to back it up with their behavior. John the Baptist calls on those presenting themselves for baptism to "bear fruits in keeping with repentance" (Matt. 3:8; Luke 3:8). Moreover, the apostle Paul in his defense before Agrippa testified that he called on his hearers to "repent and turn to God, performing deeds appropriate to repentance" (Acts 26:20). While change of behavior is not a prerequisite for forgiveness, there is the expectation that those who have accessed God's forgiveness through repentance will live differently.

Few would argue that refusal to forgive is wrong and that forgiveness in response to repentance is the most ideal, but this puts the victim in a dilemma: What is she supposed to do if there is no repentance? Is the victim risking ongoing resentment (identified in Chapter 3 as appropriate but still potentially damaging) while she is waiting for the offender to repent? What if the offender never repents? Does this mean the victim must live in a state of unforgiveness and risk all of the bad side effects mentioned earlier?

Option 3: Cheap Forgiveness

The most common (but not best) way out according to Spring is *cheap forgiveness*, which is unilateral, unconditional, and does not require anything on the part of the offender. It is also the form of forgiveness most commonly advocated by the majority of forgiveness writers, although by a different name.* It is cheap because it does not cost much for the offended and costs nothing for the offender. It is also cheap because it does not really resolve anything. Even if there is a mutual "airing out of differences," this often does not lead to a deepened relationship but rather to continued relational distance and ambivalence. The relationship, if it continues at all, tends to be awkward. Augsberger, on the other hand, claims that "Reconciliation must end in celebration, or the process has not ended. . . . To end a reconciliation negatively—'May God help us that this never happens again'—blocks our growth as persons."[2]

There are many reasons why most forgiveness writers and victims opt for this cheap imitation of real forgiveness. First, on the surface it is empowering to the victim. Now she can actually *do* something in response to what happened to her. She can forgive. Related to this sense of empowerment is the fact that nothing is required by the offender so the process cannot be derailed or aborted by the offender's refusal to recognize or admit his wrongdoing. Finally, it allows the victim to move on, hopefully with a little less anger and resentment.

---

* It is very similar to the therapeutic forgiveness criticized by L. Gregory Jones in Chapter 1.

However, the problems with this approach are numerous. Because there is no confession on the part of the offender, there is no agreement that what was done was wrong. By not repenting, the offender continues to send the secondary degrading messages mentioned in Chapter 3. Moreover, the victim still has to deal with the urge to reinterpret reality to make sense of the offender's unwillingness to confess. And finally, because the offender is still unsafe, the relationship is still strained. Thus, under the assumption that doing something is better than doing nothing, cheap forgiveness might provide some sense of comfort for the victim, but leaves the deeper issues of forgiveness unaddressed.

Option 4: Acceptance

So far, there seem to be no good options if the offender does not repent. If cheap forgiveness is not the answer to the forgiveness dilemma, what is? The way out, according to Spring, is acceptance. By acceptance, she advocates that the victim accept the fact that the offender wronged her and may never repent or even be held accountable. Once the victim can come to grips with these facts, she can re-embrace life without the ghosts from her past. Apparently, the act of accurately naming what happened has healing properties in its own right even if it is not complete forgiveness. Care must still be taken when relating to the offender (at whatever level), and the victim can say with integrity that she has done her part but due to the offender's intransigence, forgiveness is being postponed until the offender has repented and earned it.

ACCEPTANCE OR TRUST

This taxonomy by Spring is very helpful and represents a significant positive development in the theoretical understanding of forgiveness. To claim that true forgiveness requires repentance (as evidenced by offenders' change in behavior) makes forgiveness not only costly but powerful, and comes closer to the forgiveness modeled by God than much of that presented in the forgiveness literature. It is also helpful (and biblical) to be reminded that absolute refusal to forgive is not a good or healthy option.

Spring's greatest contribution is to create a space for those who want to heal but do not want to participate in cheap forgiveness. The fact that there are other options available to victims that do not involve denial or continued bitterness provides a way forward toward healing. Victims can name and then accept what happened to them and still reserve forgiveness for the day if and when their offenders repent.

The only serious concern with Spring's option of acceptance is that it does not address justice. From a Christian perspective, there are consequences for sin that, if waived, call into question the very holiness and goodness of God. According to Spring, the charges are never dropped but the victim can come to some peace about the situation even if the offender appears to have gotten away with his offense. But from a Christian perspective, there can be no "getting away with it" or God's character is called into question.

One of the advantages of Spring's view of genuine forgiveness is that it begins with a validation of the victim by means of the offender's repentance. But while the victim longs for such validation, the offender does not need to be the *only one* who can grant it. Is it possible that some third party or judge who stands above *both* victim and offender could validate the victim by taking her side of the story? And could this alternative validation be available apart from the offender's recognition of it? Furthermore, if this judgment is indeed higher than both victim and offender, the judge would then be in a position to exact justice. This is great news to the victim, if the judge validates her side of the story.

Of course, this is exactly what is available to the Christian. If a wrong has been committed, it is not only validating to know that the victim is seeing the situation correctly, but it is also comforting to know that the offender will one day pay for what he has done. There will be no getting away with it. Therefore, the believer does not merely have to stoically *accept* the situation, but she can actively rest in the assurance that the God of all justice will one day make things right. I remember hearing a speaker talk about several incidences in his life when justice was miscarried. He ended his talk by informing the audience, "I am continually comforted by the fact that God keeps score." Nobody gets away with anything with God and this is great comfort for victims. I would suggest the term for this approach would be "trust."

Thus the resentment referred to in Chapter 3 could be seen more accurately as a longing for justice. The best way to reduce such resentment or indignation is to find some confidence that justice will be served. Knowing this allows the heart of the victim to loosen. In this case, the need to face and respond to ongoing unrepentance can be referred to the superior court with assurance that justice will be done. Unlike human courts where justice can be bought or misdirected, God's rendering will always be fair in light of a comprehensive assessment of all of the evidence. It is in light of this that victims can trust in the God of justice and not just accept their lot. Furthermore, I believe that trust, rather than mere acceptance, affords a better foundation for healing.

ROMANS 12:9–21

Trust is the basis of true unilateral healing for victims. This is why Romans 12:9–21 is a key passage on the subject of healing from others' wrongs against us, for it deals very directly with the resentment that arises and often persists as a result of interpersonal sin. Again, if this resentment poses a barrier to genuine forgiveness (when the offender repents), then it needs to be explored and somehow addressed seriously. But if this resentment is merely an appropriate emotional reaction to sin yet to be addressed, then healing can only come by means of some assurance that one day justice will be complete and final.

The twelfth chapter of Romans begins the so-called "practical section" of the book.* After eleven chapters of theology, Paul "urges" his readers to live out their lives in light of the gospel he has just outlined. After encouraging his readers to renew their minds (12:1–2) and benefit from each other's gifts (12:3–8), Paul takes up the subject of relationships. It is in this context that Paul addresses dealing with the resentment that results from others' sin. It is important to note that the passage begins with a command to "let love be without hypocrisy" (v. 9). Whatever loves means in this text, there is no place for pretending or reconstructing reality. Good and evil not only remain distinct categories but one is to be adored and the other is to be abhorred. This is the affective element mentioned earlier. It is difficult to imagine generating a hatred for evil, if evil is a fluid construct based on a cognitive reframe. In other words, if someone hurt me because of a misunderstanding, for example, then abhorring what he did seems like an overreaction. Only if what he did was evil, and I recognize it as such, is resentment the proper response.

---

* Granted, these divisions are simplistic. There is a lot of theology in the so-called "practical section," and the so-called "theological section" has many practical implications also.

Verses 10–16 expand on what this means when applied to interpersonal relationships. The default setting is to be one of love, respect, humility, and generosity as these traits relate to others. Following these admonitions would go a long way toward preventing many of the interpersonal problems that invariably emerge in any group of sinners. However, in some cases, there will be conflict. When this conflict arises, the response must be both moral and justifiable.

One possible response is revenge. When we are hurt, the strong urge is to hurt back and thus even the score. In a world where justice rarely prevails, the temptation to take justice into our own hands is very appealing. The thought of repaying our offenders (usually in a way that overcompensates for the damage of the original hurt) seems to provide comfort as we painfully watch the ones who hurt us go on with their lives as if nothing happened. However, Romans 12:17 forbids this choice. God's people are not allowed to pay back evil for evil. The reason revenge is forbidden in this passage is that we are being watched. Thus we are always to conduct ourselves in such a way that "is right in the sight of all men" (v. 17b).

But there are further problems beyond the biblical mandate to refrain from revenge. The main drawback of revenge fantasies is that they are seldom satisfactory when fulfilled. Deep inside we know that revenge will only leave a bitter taste in our mouths. Revenge also does not ultimately vindicate the original victim; it merely indicates that the victim has somehow found the resources and will to act against the original offender. It could be said that revenge is an issue of power, not justice. In contrast to revenge, what victims *really* long for is for someone else, *someone above both offender and victim*, to take the victims' side and execute justice upon the offenders.

Not only are we to abstain from revenge, but we are also not to be easily offended in the first place. Christians are not to be professional victims, always clamoring for their supposed rights, but rather are to do whatever is necessary, so far as it is within their control, to "be at peace with all men" (v. 18). Again, since Christians are to abhor evil (v. 9), the ability to diagnose evil must remain intact. However, there is no place for someone with a "chip on his shoulder," always ready for a confrontation. "So far as it depends on you" indicates that sometimes conflict will remain, despite our best efforts to resolve it. It is in these cases, in which the offender will not repent, that both appropriate and inappropriate resentment can set in.

If revenge is not an option, then it seems the victim is left with one of two unpleasant options: blame herself or accept that justice is only a myth. Blaming ourselves only degrades our radars, as mentioned earlier; and abandoning a sense of justice only leads to despair. However, verse 19 introduces a new option. By refraining from personal revenge, the victims can actually get out of God's way. God is still the righteous Judge of the universe and He sees everything. Furthermore, sin still makes Him angry. He, more than anyone else, abhors evil (v. 9b). Any just punishment that the victim could ever imagine is nothing compared to the sentence given by God. Thus the victim is urged to "leave room" for God's wrath. This is because God reserves vengeance to Himself. Note that God does not condemn vengeance or portray it as inherently wrong. Rather, He assures victims that *He*, the righteous and all-powerful Judge, will see to it.

This statement of God's ownership of vengeance is not new. In Romans 12, Paul cites Moses' farewell speech in Deuteronomy 32, (specifically v. 35), where God assures His people that their oppressors would one day be called to answer for their deeds. God can guarantee this because He is the ultimate righteous Judge. "His work is perfect, for all His ways are just; a God of faithfulness and without injustice, righteous and upright is He" (Deut. 32:4).

And how does this righteous Judge respond to evil? First, He sees it all and nothing is forgotten. Put another way, God keeps score (Deut. 32:35a). Furthermore, His sense of justice is outraged with the behavior that He witnesses. God is not shy about how He feels about sin, declaring, "For a fire is kindled in My anger, and burns to the lowest parts of Sheol, and consumes the earth with its yield, and sets on fire the foundations of the mountains" (Deut. 32:22). Needless to say, God is not indifferent to evil. He clearly does not "accept" it, but rather His anger burns against it. To use theological language, this is the "wrath of God," or to use the language of Chapter 3, He resents it strongly.

It is thus God's holiness that assures that every bit of His wrath is just. Therefore, God alone can be trusted with vengeance which, from His perspective, is merely a synonym for justice. Only God has the moral superiority to stand in judgment of everybody else. And because He is holy, He will not let evil win. Lest the reader think that God is speaking only in eloquent metaphors, God vividly describes what His vengeance looks like in Deuteronomy 32:41–42: "If I sharpen My flashing sword, and My hand takes hold on justice, I will render vengeance on My adversaries, and I will repay those who hate me. I will make My arrows drunk with blood, and My sword shall devour flesh, with the blood of the slain and the captives."

By God reserving vengeance for Himself, He takes the burden of justice off of the victim's shoulders. In contrast, Spring shifts the burden from victim to offender. But if the offender will not repent and make things right, the burden of justice is shifted to the ultimate Judge who reserves vengeance for Himself. Knowing that evil will one day be judged and destroyed allows the victim to legitimately counter the hostile messages sent to her by the offender's nonrepentance. Someone above them both *will* render a verdict and His judgment will stand, as God promises in Romans 12:19: "I will repay."

As strange as it is to our ears, the contemplation of God executing vengeance upon the unjust is actually a cause for celebration. Again, in Deuteronomy 32:43, the people are called to *rejoice* when God avenges them. If it is morally permissible, even called for, to rejoice at the just destruction of the wicked, is it not equally permissible to pray to that end? Is that not what every supplicant is asking for when the petition is voiced, "Thy kingdom come"? Not only are these types of prayers permissible but they are preserved and modeled in Scripture. These sections of Scripture are commonly referred to in the collective as the imprecatory psalms, and they give voice to the cry of victims for divine justice.

CHAPTER 6

TRUSTING GOD FOR JUSTICE

The righteous will rejoice when he sees the vengeance; He will wash his feet in the blood of the wicked.
—Psalm 58:10

I will never forget one of the first stories of sexual abuse that I ever heard. As Rachel's narrative unfolded, my heart sank to hear what her perpetrator did to her. She concluded her story with this haunting question, "Where is God in all of this? I feel like He has abandoned me." At the time, having recently received a master's degree in biblical counseling, I thought I should provide some kind of scriptural encouragement. Thinking that a reminder of God's presence might be helpful, I suggested she meditate on Hebrews 13:5 and celebrate that God will never leave her or forsake her. She was respectful, but unimpressed. For if God were really with her all the time, she asked, why did He let it happen in the first place? I was out of answers at that point, and our session came to a close.

A few weeks later I noticed a bit more life in her face and something that seemed like hope. When I questioned her, she said she had been reading her Bible and that it was having a powerfully encouraging effect on her. Sure that it was my skill in navigating Scripture that had helped, I asked her what she had been reading. To my great surprise she replied, "The book of Revelation." I must confess that of all of the books in Scripture that I might use to bring comfort to a sexual-abuse victim, a book full of prophecies about war, earthquakes, blood, and beasts with brutal powers does not come to mind first.

When I asked why the book of Revelation had meant so much to her, she said, "Because someone is going to pay for what was done to me." This answer has stuck with me all of these years and has helped me see the link between comfort and a longing for justice.

Perhaps nowhere in Scripture is this longing for justice more poignantly expressed than in the imprecatory psalms. The word "imprecatory" means "to call down curses upon," and so this section of the Bible consists of individuals and groups pleading with God to pour out justice on those who have mistreated them and/or their God.

IMPRECATORY PSALMS

Although traditionally, ten specific psalms have been classified as imprecatory (7, 35, 55, 58, 59, 69, 79, 109, 137, and 139), cries for God's vengeance and judgment are frequent throughout the Psalter (28:4; 52:5; and 68:1–2). There are several scholarly definitions and classifications of the imprecatory psalms, but it is agreed that some portions of many psalms and some whole psalms have as their theme a petitioner asking for the just destruction of an enemy or perpetrator. This destruction is anticipated with joy and sometimes it is as if the writer is actually comforted by the thought that one day justice will be served. Now on the surface, these psalms seem to sound a different tone than what we are used to reading, in both the Psalter specifically and the Bible in general. For this reason, some authors have expressed concerns with the imprecatory psalms.

Concerns with Imprecatory Psalms

Concern #1. The first concern is that the language of the imprecatory psalms is too violent. For example, how could a loving God endorse such brutal phrases as: "shatter their teeth in their mouth" (58:6), and "Blessed will be those who dash your little ones against a rock" (137:9)? Does God really intend for His people to pray this way?

Some have attempted to respond to this concern by explaining that the language of these particular psalms is culturally dated and thus should be taken with a grain of salt. In the era in which these psalms were written, it was customary for people not only to wipe out their enemies, but also to exterminate their whole families, as is mentioned in Psalm 109:9–13. Hence, it would be natural for people of that day to speak like this, but contemporary readers are not to take this language literally (so the argument goes). While the cultural issues relevant to the original writing of Scripture always need to be considered, evangelicals believe that the Bible also proclaims a timeless, true narrative in the midst of the culturally and historically fixed storylines of its characters. Once a portion of Scripture is disconnected from the rest of Scripture based on cultural grounds, the entire narrative becomes suspect, for who is to say what is culturally irrelevant and what is timeless? If the Bible is littered with mere historical trivia, why has it been preserved in such form down through the ages? These are all large hermeneutical questions that relate to more than just a few psalms asking God to honor some pretty harsh requests. While these issues are complex, if "all Scripture is inspired *and* profitable," as Paul claims in 2 Timothy 3:16 (emphasis added), then in some way, every part of the Bible is still relevant and cannot be discarded in the name of cultural or historical issues. So then, the imprecatory psalms are part of God's message to us today and we are thus called to embrace them and deal with what they say.

A second explanation for this type of extreme language comes from psychology. Perhaps the authors of the psalms are engaging in what the counseling world refers to as *catharsis*, a verbal vomiting out of the toxic, emotional waste that is infecting us from the inside. Counselors encourage this process as a powerful prerequisite to healing, for once the emotional poison has been extracted, real healing can begin. But during this catharsis, the client may express herself in ways that are uncharacteristically vulgar, melodramatic, or even brutal. While these eruptions are viewed as a valid representation of how the client is feeling *at the moment*, they are not seen as the client's *final answer*. Their validity is thus temporary. Yes, this is how the client feels *now*, but it is not how she *will* feel or *should* feel once this technique is successfully accomplished. So perhaps the psalmists are merely documenting where they were emotionally during a catharsis. Maybe what we have is a record of where David's heart and mind were going during some intensely passionate episodes. Regardless, seen from this perspective, Scripture is only recording how the authors *felt at the time*, while not endorsing those feelings as a permanent posture. In other words, it is acceptable during therapy for a client to give voice to her unconscious longing for her perpetrator to pay. But she should not stay with that position. It has a short shelf life, although there is no definitive answer as to how long this shelf life is. However, similar to the cultural argument, this too requires the interpreter to pick and choose which phrases are a result of catharsis (and thus not desired as a final position), and which phrases represent the divinely endorsed and approved emotional reactions.

If these explanations are found wanting, could it be that the language is actually *not* too strong if understood properly? Maybe these harsh words are exactly the words the authors meant to be preserved. Maybe the language is not that extreme after all. Though at first glance it seems otherwise, there are two reasons that such language might not be excessive.[1]

First, the authors of the imprecatory psalms take seriously the stark difference between good and evil (and the mortal battle between them; see the treatment of Romans 12:9 in Chapter 5). In order for good to prevail, evil must be defeated, and evil will not succumb easily or quickly. In biblical times, the "kill or be killed" form of battle was intimate and bloody. In order to destroy an enemy, a person had to get close to him and attempt to deliver a lethal blow, while at the same time try to avoid being killed himself. Living in such a context would surely shape how people chose to speak. Those who are in the heat of the battle often speak in a heated way. This is where their hearts are, so this is what their mouths must speak.[2] To petition God to destroy my enemy might sound brutal to ears enjoying peace and security, but to a soldier in battle, it means victory and thus reflects the desire of his heart.

The second justification for the language in such psalms is that they are directed toward God. Thus the psalmists feel the freedom to unburden themselves in a way that, in the presence of anyone other than God, would make them feel uncomfortable. With God, they do not have to pull any punches. If the psalmists feel it, they give voice to it. Not only does God tolerate such language, but He also encourages it. This is a major theme throughout the psalms, not just those of an imprecatory nature. Consider, for example, Psalm 88, within which it is difficult after the first verse to find anything positive about anything or anyone, including God. The moral of this psalm seems to be, "If there is nothing good to say, don't try to say something good!" There is no "five steps to dealing with depression" here. The psalm does not end with a neat and tidy resolution. Rather, it ends on a dark note: "You have removed lover and friend far from me; my acquaintances are in darkness" (v. 18).

We need to become comfortable with lamentation (such as Psalm 88), even its most severe forms like those occurring in the imprecatory psalms. The existence of such psalms assures us that we can take whatever we are facing and feeling in life to God. We can run to Him with it, and we do not always have to be careful about how we say it to Him, as long as we are bringing it to Him (even if we bring the same thing to Him for years). That is what psalms do.[3] Thus, in light of the authors taking good and evil seriously and addressing their concerns to God, the language might not be that extreme after all.

Concern #2. While the primary concern about the imprecatory psalms is the violent language, a second related concern is that these psalms come close to advocating some kind of revenge. Whether the text actually calls for the severe actions mentioned, there is a clear longing for some kind of payback for wrongs committed (i.e., Pss. 35 and 55). From a psychological perspective, is it healthy to meditate on the destruction of our enemies? Were the psalmists brooding on past offenses? Were they preoccupied with revenge? Could they not move on with their lives? How often did they pray such prayers? The "How long, Oh Lord?" of Psalm 13:1 seems to indicate that these prayers were voiced more than once. If Christian counselors used these psalms with clients, might we be risking slowing down their healing, or even worse, fostering a bitter spirit of revenge?

The response to this concern is to recognize the difference between revenge and a longing for justice. On the surface it may appear difficult to differentiate between these two ideas but they are not the same. One difference is that revenge is usually orchestrated or committed by the victim, whereas justice is rendered by someone other than the victim. A more profound difference is that vigilante justice or revenge does not necessarily validate the victim; it merely inflicts pain on the offender. This is why revenge is so dangerous and dissatisfying. True justice, on the other hand, is executed by someone *above* both victim and offender who is in a position to render a judgment. When the judge renders a verdict in favor of the victim, this *does* validate the victim (assuming of course that the judge is fair and understands the evidence). If this is all true, then justice is a much higher desire than mere revenge. This is part of the warning against revenge in Romans 12, mentioned in Chapter 5.

Imagine the reassurance if the supreme Judge were to say, "Vengeance is mine and I will repay." This promise not only assures the victim that what happened to her was witnessed, but also guarantees that a verdict has been rendered and the offender has been pronounced guilty and deserving of punishment. This might explain some of the popularity of the television shows that focus on cold cases (cases that remain unsolved after a long period of time). Often during such shows, detectives admit being motivated by the idea that they "work for God." The idea is that regardless of the length of time that the case has been unresolved, God has not forgotten and is still pursuing justice. In my local police station hangs a poster asking for information about a man who was murdered and left in the park almost twenty years ago. Sometimes I wonder if anyone even remembers who that person was anymore. But God does. And God knows who killed him. Someday, justice will be rendered in this case. Even though I have no idea who this person was, I can take great comfort that the God of the universe has not forgotten and will one day close this case.

Ironically, while contemporary commentators stumble over the vivid language, many of the original authors actually derived comfort from the thought of justice being administered and evil being violently defeated. They not only looked forward to the relief from their current persecution and suffering by the destruction of the evildoers, but they actually anticipated God being glorified through the defeat of the wicked. It would be one thing to make rash statements in the heat of the moment; it is quite another to put these thoughts in writing under the supervision of the Holy Spirit. More seems to be going on here than mere vindictive revenge. The authors are not just fantasizing about the destruction of someone who hurt them; they are crying out to a just, holy, and all-powerful God, asking Him to do what is right.

> The righteous will rejoice when he sees the vengeance; He will wash his feet in the blood of the wicked. And men will say, "Surely there is a reward for the righteous; surely there is a God who judges on earth!" (Ps. 58:10–11).

ROLE OF THE IMPRECATORY PSALMS
IN FORGIVENESS COUNSELING

Even though I believe there is a very helpful role for the imprecatory psalms in forgiveness work, I do not want to revert to the concordance method of using Scripture. "Read this passage and you will feel better" is a reckless use of Scripture. However, if the client feels that the harsh language of the imprecatory psalms gives her a voice, she may be more receptive to what the rest of Scripture has to say. If I am correct about all of the inner turmoil churning within a victim, I believe that the imprecatory psalms give a divinely inspired language to the offended party's righteous longing for justice. Thus, the primary goal of having clients read the imprecatory psalms is not to give them a treatment plan for what to do to feel better. Rather it is to validate and give voice to the cry for justice in their hearts. This in turn contributes to their healing, which is the more desirable goal.

This longing for justice is neither pathological nor sinful. It alone does not create ulcers or distance us from God. The longing is for justice, not revenge. As I said earlier, having a judge declare the verdict in my favor is much more satisfying than trying to execute revenge on my own. Justice includes validation. It is as if God is saying, "*Your radar is correct. Something horrible did happen to you and I saw it happen. My memory is photographic, comprehensive, and perfect. I will not forget.*" Once again, God keeps score.

A second benefit from reading the imprecatory psalms is the reassurance that not only does God see everything that happened but He *will* do something about it. He not only has the power (omnipotence) and the authority (holiness) but He also has the will and the motivation to do something about injustice. Because of the assurance that God will address the issue, the victim is released from the responsibility. Remember God's admonition in Romans 12:19 to "leave room for the wrath of God." Once the victim is convinced that justice will occur, there is no longer any need to explain away why justice has not happened yet. Again, perhaps God is saying something to the effect, "*Not only did I see what happened to you; I will see that justice is done. One day your offender will have to answer to me. That will be a good day for you as it will validate what you have known all along. Because you can trust me to take care of what happened to you, you can stop damaging yourself with unhelpful and untrue cognitive reframes.*"

Finally, since the imprecatory psalms were originally prayers, they can also serve as a template for contemporary prayers for justice. With all of the painful stories that we hear, even we as counselors can struggle with whether God is truly on the side of justice. As we routinely try to help our clients deal with injustice, there can be a subtle temptation to resign ourselves to the view that the God of justice is somehow off-duty. We begin to expect evil to win and to conclude that God, while caring a great deal about healing, does not care that much about justice.

So maybe praying the imprecatory psalms is not only helpful for the client but also might be of great benefit to the counselor. How often do we as counselors pray that a predator will be caught and judged accurately? I remember once being part of a special prayer meeting of a group of counselors asking God to ordain that a sexual predator was convicted and sentenced in an upcoming trial. Needless to say, this was not the standard type of prayer meeting to which I was accustomed. This type of praying may seem odd, but to be like Jesus is to be like God, and God is a god of justice. That is part of His love. We cannot say we love others if we do not stand for justice on their behalf. Yes, it is surely appropriate to pray that God would heal; but it is equally appropriate to pray that He would execute justice or vengeance, especially when He promised that He would. This is why God's people, no matter the circumstances, may be helpless but they are not hopeless. They can always cry out for God's ultimate vindication of Himself and His people. It is this cry that is given language in the imprecatory psalms.

CHAPTER 7

IMPACT OF THE IMPRECATORY PSALMS

And men will say, "Surely there is a reward for the
righteous; surely there is a God who judges on earth!"
—Psalm 58:11

To summarize my views on the imprecatory psalms from the previous chapter: 1) They are part of inspired Scripture; 2) the language used is not as extreme as might be initially thought; and 3) they were preserved to give words to the timeless longing for justice in a world where evil and sin win most of the time. My reason for such a lengthy treatment of the language of the imprecatory psalms is to address what might serve as an initial distraction. But once the strong language is understood, the real impact from the imprecatory psalms comes from reading them and feeling the emotional punch of their words. The imprecatory psalms are part of a larger genre of poetry, and poetry, unlike a legal document, is aimed specifically at the emotions. So if strong feelings are triggered while reading these psalms, then that is the whole point. Space prohibits looking at every one of the imprecatory psalms but a closer look at a few particular psalms highlights three aspects of this genre that can be of theological and clinical value.

Praying for Justice Is the Proper Response to Interpersonal Sin — Psalm 7

This is the first of the recognized imprecatory psalms. Not much is known about the background story other than that, according to the title, it was written by David in response to a slander against him by a member of the royal family (Saul, of the tribe of Benjamin and family of Cush, was king at the time). Because God is a god of justice, David feels safe in appealing his case to Him. First, he opens himself to any evidence that the slander was true (vv. 3–5). Banking on the fact that God knew every detail of the case, David challenges God (and anyone else) to produce any proof that what was being said about him was correct. He is perfectly willing to let God turn the searchlight on him to see if there is any evidence, knowing that in this case, there is none. Because David is telling the truth, and he knows that God knows he is telling the truth, he fully expects there to be no answer to his challenge. Thus, the charges against David are groundless. To put this in psychological terms, the slander against David was a challenge to the accuracy of David's radar.

But establishing his innocence before God is not enough. David wants to be vindicated publicly and thus his accuser needs not only to be discredited but also to be held accountable for his sin. Here David is not being petulant, but rather mirroring in a small fashion the anger and rage that he expects from a righteous God who has had His law blatantly flouted. God remains a righteous and just judge but He also "has indignation every day" (v. 11). God is not emotionally indifferent to sin; rather, to use language from Chapter 3, He resents it greatly.

But God does not immediately destroy David's accuser. Judgment is truly coming (verse 12 says the bow is drawn and ready to shoot), but it is contingent upon the offender's nonrepentance. Here David's accuser makes his situation a lot worse by refusing to confess his sin and repent. His level of deceit and falsehood is compared to the development in the womb and eventual birth of a child (v. 14). This was no accidental stumbling into a lie, from which the offender could quickly extract himself by a quick apology. This was a deliberate act of deception that required time and planning. A similar metaphor is used in the next verse (v. 15), in which David's accuser "dug a pit," only to fall into the very trap that he set for another.

To put this psalm in the language of the levels of damage mentioned in Chapter 3, first, David's accuser slandered him. Then he complicated the damage by stubbornly refusing to repent. As long as this persisted, David was no doubt tempted to wonder if he were actually guilty of something (i.e., David felt pressure to cognitively reframe the situation so it would make sense). Finally, this would negatively affect whatever relationship David had not only with this individual but also with the entire royal family.

In response, David calls out for justice. And he does so in very emotional terms. Part of the reason David's cries for justice seem odd to modern ears is because we have been conditioned to view strong feelings as toxic. If we were David's counselors, we might be more concerned with his emotional overreaction (particularly anger) than we would the damage that was done to him. But throughout this psalm, whether David is complaining about injustice or calling on God to expose his accuser, his highly vivid and emotional language is never condemned. God does not tell David to go to his room and calm down until he can control himself. Nor does David give any hint that he is ashamed of his feelings. David's emotional language is not his problem; it is the sin that was committed against him that is the real problem.

This is an important point to emphasize. A common dictum in psychology is that although you cannot choose your circumstances, you can choose how you respond to your circumstances. While there is great wisdom in looking before you leap, it is doubtful that the distance between cognitive recognition and emotional reaction is that great. For example, a parent drives up to his house only to see it on fire. Immediately he charges in to rescue his young child who was playing inside. Was this response a well-thought-out choice or a logical reaction given the pre-existing feelings that the parent had for his child? Most parents would not say they made a choice to try to rescue their children; they just reacted. In similar fashion, our moral tastes should be so developed that we do not have to cognitively process whether something is wrong or not; rather, based on our pre-existing affections, we immediately recognize evil for what it is and react with an appropriate emotional response.

To people who have been victimized by others, this psalm provides reassuring language with which to voice their very legitimate complaints. It must be noted that David does not pray that God would help him *forgive* his offender (in contrast to most forgiveness literature). Nor does he ask God to help him accept the situation and move on (in contrast to Spring's model mentioned earlier). Rather, he pleads for a holy God to do right, which is to vindicate David and expose his accuser's sin. If David, a man after God's own heart, can pray like this, so can we. Thus, it is not wrong for an abuse victim to pray that her abuser will be exposed and that justice will be done. Praying this way in faith can be very therapeutic for the client as these prayers continually reinforce not only the truth of the situation, but also the legitimate longing for justice.

Hatred for Sin Is the Proper Motivation behind a Desire for Justice — Psalm 139:19–22

One of the reasons that I chose Psalm 139 is that much of this psalm is well known. The reassurance of God's omnipresent awareness at the beginning of the psalm lays the groundwork for the concluding call to self-examination. In the midst of outlining just how much God does know, we read one of the most famous pro-life passages in Scripture. The main point is that if God knows every detail of our lives, including even our conceptions, He can be depended on to be involved with us throughout our lives. Before concluding the psalm with another call for introspection, the psalmist appears to get distracted with a plea that this all-knowing, all-present God would slay the wicked whom the psalmist "hates." Given this abrupt change in tone, a few observations are in order.

First, as in other imprecatory psalms, the author is asking God to *slay* the wicked. What right does the author have to make such a request of God? Is the author treating God like some kind of divine hitman who is available for hire to murder his enemies? I do not think this is the case. The objects of destruction in the passage are God's enemies, and therefore by extension also enemies of the author of the psalm. But first and foremost they have spoken against God and disrespected His name. This is what has the psalmist so upset. Someone who disrespects God deserves punishment (Exod. 20:7), and the author is merely reminding God of this.

Second, the psalmist does not stop with just a cognitive recognition that a grievous sin has been committed. He goes on to admit that anyone who treats his God that way is an object of hatred to him. This is a strong emotional response and in case there is any confusion, the psalmist uses several synonyms and even admits hating with the "utmost hatred" those who disrespect God. It seems that the psalmist is more upset by how the wicked treat God than he is by how the wicked might treat him.

Again, it might be easy to stumble over the language here. When is it ever permissible to hate someone? Especially in current culture, no one wants to be labeled a "hater." Did Jesus not say that the posture of "love your neighbor and hate your enemy" is out of date (Matt. 5:43–44)? Maybe the answer has to do with *why* someone is an object of hatred. In this psalm, it is those who hate God who consequently become objects of the author's hatred (v. 21). It is God's enemies who are identified as worthy of hatred by all who love God. Perhaps meditating on the greatness of God makes anything other than reverent worship of Him repellent to the author.

This admission of hatred also challenges the often-cited distinction of loving the sinner but hating the sin. Here it seems that the author hates both the sin and the sinner. Could the hatred referred to here be another term for the legitimate emotional reaction to the cognitive recognition of something genuinely horrible? Or is the psalmist merely using the word "hatred" to say that he resents the attitudes and behaviors of the wicked? Finally, just because the psalmist is experiencing a strong emotional reaction to the wicked does not mean that he has to act on these feelings. He could be full of legitimate rage and still willingly step aside to leave room for the wrath of God, who promised, "Vengeance is mine, I will repay." If someone deserves to answer for his crimes, would we not prefer that he answer to the almighty God of the universe?

Regardless of the use of the word "hatred" in this psalm, the author seems not the least bit uneasy about speaking this way. After admitting that he hates God's enemies with the utmost hatred (v. 22), he shifts to petitioning God to search his heart to see if there is any of that evil in him. Only the omniscient God whom the author praised at the beginning of the psalm would be capable of such a revealing search. So it is possible to celebrate and worship an all-knowing God (and even request that He shine His light on our soul), while at the same time respond with strong feelings to those who hate such a God and practice injustice.

Two other passages reinforce this point that it is someone's loyalties and behavior that make him an object of legitimate hate. David claims in Psalm 31:6, "I hate those who regard vain idols; but I trust in the Lord." For the Old Testament Jews, worshiping idols was not just an alternative religious choice. It was a direct statement against the true God who had laid a claim to their loyalty since the covenant of Abraham. Thus it was a betrayal. To anyone who loved God, those who were traitors to Him would deserve strong negative feelings, such as hatred.

Similarly, Psalm 119:158 (NIV) says, "I look on the faithless with loathing, for they do not obey your word." Here again, the author is not just a hateful person but is reserving his hatred for those who are faithless and those who refuse to obey God. There is no mere neutrality in Scripture. Turning away from God always involves turning toward something else—something that, is in the long run, disgusting and repulsive.

Rejoicing in the Destruction of Evil Is a Proper Response to Justice — Psalm 58

There is a huge irony in that this psalm is a complaint to the divine Judge about the injustice of human judges. The background is unclear but it seems that those who were expected to render righteous verdicts were actually perverting the very justice they were called to uphold. The author goes so far as to accuse them of justifying violence (v. 2) by means of deception, which for them was as natural as a birthmark (v. 3). Evil people lie and their lies hurt. This resonates with the message communicated by nonrepentance mentioned earlier. Whatever excuse the offender gives (especially if he stubbornly persists with this excuse) is another blow to the victim because if the offender's view is correct, then somehow the victim's interpretation of things must be clouded. Again, if someone's radar proves to be faulty on a regular basis, eventually it is no longer consulted.

It is important to note that the focus of this text, while mentioning the original offense, seems to be on the intransigent lies of and cover-up by the offenders. The offenders are dangerous and deaf (perhaps to invitations to repent), a deadly combination. Thus, the author asks God to break through the lies and render the offenders' deceit powerless. If the offenders are really a "deaf cobra" (v. 4), then there is no rationalizing with it. It must be defanged or destroyed.

Verses 6–8 contain some of the most vivid language in the imprecatory psalms. Verse 6 requests that God render the offenders powerless by means of breaking their teeth out. Whether the metaphor is of a lion or a cobra, either way, removing their teeth greatly reduces their ability to cause harm. The author follows up this request with a plea that the wicked would not only be rendered powerless but that they would be eliminated. One metaphor is that of a snail trying to move in hot sun, which probably represents God thwarting the plans of the wicked once they are in motion. The next metaphor of a miscarriage asks that God prevent the plans of the wicked from ever being completed, even after they are already begun.

In verse 9, the psalmist prays that this justice would not only occur but occur quickly. No one likes to wait for water to boil, especially if he is watching the pot closely. Similarly, no victim likes to wait for justice even though she watches for it every day. I have worked with several victims of childhood abuse whose perpetrators seemed to have avoided justice for decades. This is hard to endure. Prayers for swift justice continue as victims look forward to the day of reckoning.

Finally, and this is perhaps one of the most unexpected twists of the psalm, the author claims that watching (but not participating in) the vengeance of God will be an occasion to celebrate (vv. 10–11). While the method of celebration (splashing around in the blood of his ene-mies) may seem a bit gory, it does signify total and utter defeat. Verse 11 explains the real reason for such joy. It is not just that David survived and his enemies did not. It was that the destruction of evil is always a reminder that "there is a God who judges on earth!" Witnessing the destruction of the wicked at the hands of a righteous judge gives a temporary foretaste of what will one day be permanent and total destruction of the wicked, and that indeed will be a great day. I have been to a few movies where I have witnessed spontaneous applause in the theater when the villain is defeated by the hero (or yet another Death Star is destroyed). Even in this sterile setting, where both hero and villain are actors and neither will ever hear the applause, there still exists a kind of visceral joy even when imaginary evil is thwarted.

Similarly, when David mentions in Psalm 35:9 that his soul will re-joice in the Lord and exult in His salvation, the occasion for this rejoic-ing is the destruction of those who were seeking to harm him (vv. 1–8). When God delivers David by letting his enemies fall into their own trap of destruction, David sees an occasion for joy. Again, when evil plans and the people who devise them are thwarted, it is a cause for celebration. We may not be comfortable with such thinking but such discomfort exposes our lack of loving what is good and hating what is evil (Rom. 12:9). When we really understand (both cognitively and emotionally) what makes evil so evil, we cannot but desire that God would utterly destroy it, and be glad when He does.

RELATIONSHIP BETWEEN IMPRECATORY PSALMS AND FORGIVENESS

Forgiveness is not really the theme of the imprecatory psalms but because forgiveness is often presented as a unilateral response to interpersonal sin, the imprecatory psalms are relevant in that they present an alternative response. Rather than praying for help to forgive, the authors of these psalms ask that God would judge the wicked, with whom the authors are thoroughly repulsed. Furthermore, when this judgment occurs, the authors are prepared to celebrate. For many of the abuse clients that I have had over the years, this is a much more liberating option than feeling pressure to forgive their offenders—a pressure that often leads more to false guilt than to freedom or healing. Most victims already struggle with the damaging cognitive reframe that what happened was somehow their fault. Their guilt is only compounded when they cannot seem to even forgive correctly. I believe this is one of the reasons cheap forgiveness does not help. It does not address the issue of justice.

On the other hand, praying through some of the imprecatory psalms not only addresses justice but makes it the main point. When I assign these passages either as homework or to be read out loud in session, clients report being pleasantly surprised that a part of Scripture captures what they are feeling so accurately. To see that David and others brought their hearts to God in a way that was real is of great comfort to those who may share the same feelings but not be comfortable voicing them.

Addressing justice also validates what the victim suspects: the problem is with the actions of the offender, not the victim's inability to forgive. When victims realize not only that justice is coming but that it is fully legitimate to pray for that day, their hearts are freed up to heal. Justice becomes the responsibility of the most righteous, all-knowing, and all-powerful Judge in the universe who can never be bought off, lose their file, or make a mistake. This frees victims to focus on their own healing, without the pressure to prematurely forgive.

CHAPTER 8

FORGIVENESS IS ACTIVE AND OTHER CENTERED

We cannot love alone and we cannot forgive alone.
—Janis Abrahms Spring

Forgiving love is the inconceivable, unexplainable pursuit of the offender by the offended for the sake of restored relationship with God, self, and others.
—Dan B. Allender and Tremper Longman

Early in my teaching career, I was a little more willing to allow students to borrow my books. Sometimes I even forgot that I had loaned them out. One day as I was walking across campus, a student approached me and after greeting me, confessed that he had borrowed one of my books a year ago and had forgotten to return it. He went on to confess that after realizing so much time had gone by, he was tempted just to keep my book, especially since I did not seem to miss it. However, he said that God was convicting him and so he sought me out and returned my book. My response that day was some kind of mumbled, "Really? I forgot that I even had that book," followed by "That's OK." The whole conversation was less than a minute long.

I have sometimes wondered if there was a better response I could have given that repentant thief. Since his confession seemed to be a result of

God's working in his life, would my response not warrant something a little more substantive than "That's OK"? What does "That's OK" even mean? What is OK? Is it OK that he took my book and did not return it? Is it OK now because he confessed and gave it back? Is our relationship now OK? And if I really did forget that I even had the book, then why should he even bother to return it? Why did I not respond with something like "That is wonderful! It is nice to have my book back but it is even more exciting to hear that God is working in your life. I forgive you"?

A little more serious example occurred early in my pastoral ministry. It was obvious that Paul was upset about something when he asked to speak with me after church. Paul was a forty-year-old man whose wife of twenty years had left him a year previous for another man. Paul faithfully brought his three kids to church every other weekend and sought counsel from both the pastor and a counselor recommended by the church. Now a year later, Paul was still grieving but was trying to live with a routine that did not include his wife. In a side office of the church Paul shared something that had happened the day before to disrupt that routine. The "other man" had unexpectedly called Paul to repent. He confessed to Paul that what he had done was wrong and he realized that his actions had caused Paul a great deal of pain and changed his life forever. He concluded by saying that he was no longer seeing Paul's wife and hoped that Paul could one day forgive him. On the phone, Paul stumbled through some response but later wished he would have had something better to say. His question to me was "What should I have said to him?" In retrospect, Paul wished he would have said something that included "I forgive you."

These two stories highlight the discomfort that often occurs when one person tries to confess a sin to another person. What do we say in such situations? Why are such conversations so awkward? Why do the words, "I forgive you" come with almost as much difficulty as "I was wrong"? One argument could be that since we so seldom confess our sins to each other, we are out of practice in how to respond when it does happen. Many of us as children were required to ask for and grant forgiveness whether we understood it or not. For example, when my boys were younger, they would sometimes settle their differences of opinion by breaking each other's toys. On one occasion, one of my sons was employing this strategy when he was caught by the ultimate authority (me). I banished him to his room until he was willing to apologize to his brother. Because the strong-willed gene is dominant in our family, this looked to be a long siege. However, after just a few minutes of this standoff, the "victim" realized he was alone with no one to play with. So he knocked on the bedroom door with this plea to his brother: "Come on, I'll forgive you; just say you're sorry." I suspect my victimized son had less than pure motives in his appeal for his brother to repent. However, he was offering something like forgiveness in response to repentance. Shortly thereafter, my guilty son did say he was sorry; the matter was dropped and they went back to playing together.

Witnessing this relatively simple example of repentance and forgiveness between my sons made me wonder how and why it becomes so complex for adults. Confessing sin is hard but receiving someone's confession can be just as difficult. When someone truly repents, he is inviting his victim to revisit the offense, and sometimes she is either not ready or would just rather not hear it. This is no doubt true but if we believe confession and repentance are good things, we should always be ready to celebrate when someone repents and turns around.

Another obstacle is that in some cases we suspect that there is more behind our offenders' confession than just repentance. We are suspicious of the authenticity of their professed confession. There is little we can do to absolutely authenticate someone's repentance (I will address this in the next chapter) but ultimately, we cannot negate all repentance in the name of self-protection. Maybe focusing too much on ourselves is part of the problem. What if when others confess their sins to us, our response should be for their benefit, not ours? If so, forgiveness is other-centered and therefore, rather than hoping uncomfortable discussions do not happen, maybe we should pursue them.

A BIBLICAL PRECEDENT: THE STORY OF JOSEPH

A biblical story that dramatizes the active and other-centered nature of forgiveness is the story of Joseph (Gen. 37–50), in which the word "forgive" appears for the first time in the Bible (Gen. 50:17). Admittedly, antecedents for the concept of forgiveness can be traced all the way back to the promises given in Genesis 3 and the substitute provided for Abraham's son in Genesis 22, so we must be careful not to put too much importance on the first occurrence. Merely the fact that the term is mentioned first in Genesis may or may not carry that much extra weight. However, the fact that the term does occur for the first time during a rich and detailed narrative about forgiveness does call for a closer look at the story.

The plot is familiar to any student of Scripture but bears repeating here to elucidate key moments that help define biblical forgiveness. Joseph was clearly the preferred son of his father Jacob and became aware of his privileged position early in his life. He alone received the multi-colored coat—a blatant statement by his father identifying the favorite son. Although only Benjamin (the other biological son of Rachel) was younger, Joseph was so confident in his position that he felt the free-dom to tattle on his older brothers and to share with them his grandiose dreams of power. Although they grew to hate him, there was little they could do (37:1–5).

Eventually the brothers had their opportunity. When Joseph was sent to check up on them, boldly wearing his coat, his brothers were not where they were supposed to be. Who knows what they were doing in Dothan and whether they feared Joseph telling on them again, but they decided this was the day they would rid themselves of their annoying favored little brother. Initially they wanted to kill him but Reuben, the eldest, utilized his influence to convince the others merely to put him in a pit. Later, when a slave trader came by, a workable solution that did not involve murder presented itself. Joseph went from favored son to powerless slave in less than a day.

Imagine the jolt to Joseph's self-identity—no more gifts, no more privileged position. And it was all done far away from his father's protec-tive and pampering influence. He probably knew that his brothers did not like him that much, but he never imagined they would contemplate selling him as a slave—not to mention killing him. After the journey to Egypt, Joseph, the previously favored one, was sold like a piece of prop-erty. His servitude was not the temporary working off of a debt; this was permanent. He now belonged to Potiphar, just like any of Potiphar's other possessions. Joseph would celebrate his next birthday as a slave with no hope of anything else for the rest of his life. He had probably enjoyed the attention of servants as a young favored boy. Now he was the servant. He must attend to someone else and defer his own desires to those of an-other. And all because his brothers could not stand that he had surpassed them all in privilege merely because of who his mother was.

Despite the radical change in station, Joseph prospered even as a slave and consequently, his master promoted him to master of his household. This meant an elevation in position for Joseph, until he was victimized by Potiphar's wife and then thrown in prison—a position worse than slavery. However, through these unpredictable fluctuations in stature, "the Lord was with Joseph" (39:2, 3, 21, 23). For at least a decade, Joseph had many opportunities to reflect on and resent what his brothers had done to him.

Finally, at age thirty, he interpreted Pharaoh's dream and was promoted to second in the kingdom. As he rode through the country seeing the people bow to him and hearing Pharaoh announce his new authority, he must have reflected on his childhood dream (37:5–11), in which he foresaw that one day his brothers and parents would bow to him. Now he witnessed that what God had said was coming true. Instead of a multi-colored coat, he had many garments of fine linen, a signet ring, and a gold necklace (41:42). If God could fulfill the dreams He had given him as a teenager, Joseph might have wondered about the part of the dream in which his brothers and even his father bowed to him. Would that come to pass also?

In addition to his newfound power and prestige, Joseph was also given a wife who bore him two sons. The names of these boys give some indication as to where Joseph was in the process of his own personal healing. He named his firstborn Manasseh, which literally means "one who causes to forget." Joseph was clear in his explanation of the name that he wanted his son to be a reminder that he had forgotten all of his trouble and his father's household (41:51). His next son was named Ephraim, which means "fruitful." Joseph not only had put his past behind him but he was actually flourishing in the land "of his affliction" (41:52). Apparently, Joseph had come to some kind of peace with what had happened to him (to use clinical language, Joseph was experiencing healing). He was thriving in his new life. Then the seven years of famine began and Joseph's peace with his past was to be tested.

Joseph's treatment of his brothers when they journeyed to Egypt for food is complex and difficult to interpret. His harsh accusations when he first recognized them could indicate an impulsive desire for revenge (42:7–8). He had them imprisoned and released all but one, to test their loyalty. However, any interpretation of Joseph's behavior as exacting vengeance must account for the repeated occurrence of his tears (42:24; 43:30; 45:2, 15).

After loading up their bags with food, Joseph insisted that Benjamin accompany them back the next time to verify that there even was a Benjamin and that he was as they said he was. When the brothers found out that one of them (Simeon) would remain confined until Benjamin was produced, they immediately began to interpret the situation as God's just punishment for their treatment of their brother long ago. Reuben added an "I told you so" (42:22).

Whether it was the voice of Reuben (the only one to vote against killing Joseph earlier) or just hearing all of his brothers admit their wrongdoing, Joseph could not contain himself and went away to weep. When he returned, he sent them on their way with their money hidden in their sacks. The brothers were stunned and dismayed to find it. They must have believed that Simeon was now doomed, and hoped they could weather the famine with what they had bought from Joseph. When Jacob was presented with the option of sending Benjamin to validate their story, he flatly refused, again favoring Rachel's descendants with his comment, "for his brother is dead, and he alone is left" (42:38).

Finally, their food ran out again and Jacob was forced to send Benjamin just to survive. Prophetically, Judah took full responsibility for Benjamin's safety as they returned to Egypt. When Joseph saw his full brother for the first time since they were children, he was overwhelmed with emotion and looked for a private place where his tears could flow. Later he returned and favored his brothers with a feast, although he could not eat at the same table with them. The brothers had reluctantly come back, so Simeon was released. But would they stand up for Benjamin, the only remaining brother from the favored wife? Joseph first tested them by giving Benjamin five times the food that was given to the others. This was an amazing statement in a time of famine. The last time the brothers had witnessed such favoritism, they had sold their brother into slavery. What would they do with Benjamin? Joseph devised a clever plan to find out.

After letting them go, he directed his men to stop them again, as his royal cup was missing. The guards found it in Benjamin's sack, but instead of using the opportunity to get rid of the last remaining favored son, the brothers all returned to Joseph. In a gesture that still drips with irony,

Joseph offered to keep Benjamin as a slave and let the rest go. Benjamin would forever be labeled as a thief and would remain an anonymous slave for the rest of his life—the same fate the brothers assumed had befallen Joseph. This offer would not even interfere with the brothers returning at a future date for more food. Also, Jacob would no longer be able to favor Rachel's sons, for they would be no more. In essence, Joseph was giving his brothers a golden opportunity to get rid of Benjamin just as they had done to him years earlier. He was even supplying the alibi.

However, the brothers had changed since their treatment of Joseph. They all stood by Benjamin—even when he was given five times more food than they had. This time they loved their father enough to keep his favorite son alive. Once again, it was Judah who stood up and made the remarkable offer to be enslaved in his brother's place. Judah would take the punishment that Benjamin supposedly deserved.*

Aside from the clear prophetic implications, Judah's behavior was just one more indication that something had changed in the hearts of these brothers. First, Simeon (maybe by volunteering) had agreed to stay the first time to protect his brothers. Then Reuben, the firstborn, had offered his sons if he did not bring Benjamin back safely. Now Judah was offering himself as a slave to protect Benjamin, of all people! This was not the same group of men who earlier sold their favored brother into slavery. This was what Joseph had been looking for all along. Now he was ready to reveal himself to his brothers. They had repented. Although the actual word for forgiveness is not used until Genesis 50:17, it is clear that Joseph's brothers recognized that what they did was wrong, felt remorse, and had even changed their behavior. However, years later they feared that their early betrayal would never be forgotten or forgiven (50:17ff). They even went so far as to claim that their father's dying wish was that Joseph would forgive them. In response, Joseph became very emotional, and wept yet again. To his brothers' plea for mercy, he replied,

"Do not be afraid, for am I in God's place? And as for you, you meant evil against me, but God meant it for good in order to bring about this present result, to preserve many people alive. So therefore,

---

* Of course, many generations later a descendant of Judah would do much the same thing on a grander scale.

do not be afraid; I will provide for you and your little ones." So he comforted them and spoke kindly to them (Gen. 50:19–21).

APPLICATIONS

What does the story of Joseph teach us about pursuing and offering forgiveness? Two main points have already been identified: 1) Joseph was *actively* pursuing his brothers; and 2) he was pursuing them for *their* best interest (i.e., he was other-centered). Joseph was prepared and desirous to forgive even before he witnessed his brothers' repentance. When they admitted their sin, Joseph responded in a way that demonstrated his readiness to forgive.

Through his tears Joseph revealed who he was and tried to reassure his brothers. He began by stating what they did: "I am your brother Joseph, whom you sold into Egypt" (Gen. 45:4). He was not condoning, justifying, or reframing their sin. After all these years, what they did to him was still wrong. This is an important point. His recognition that what they did was sin, and his hope that they would one day see it too, was actually a very other-centered posture for Joseph (or any victim) to take. The greatest need for sinners is to be forgiven and this means they need to see their own sin and repent. Reframing what happened potentially aborts this process for the offender. But with Joseph, there was no such cognitive reframe or projective empathy. Neither did he try to level the playing field by saying that his adolescent arrogance somehow warranted their sin.

However, Joseph did not stop with merely granting that his brothers were guilty of a moral violation. Put another way, he did not leave them in their sin. When he saw the fear in their faces, he told them not to be grieved or angry with themselves. He then shared with them the conclusions he had no doubt come to through his own healing process. God was sovereign and worked out all for his good. Even though their betrayal was cruel and sinful, God was working out a way to preserve His people through the famine that only He knew was coming. Reconciling God's sovereignty with human responsibility is always a complicated task. But Joseph was able to say to his brothers that their decision to sin against him was not the end of the story. God always reserves the last page for Himself. Because the trajectory of Joseph's life was subordinate to the plan and power of God, Joseph's brothers could not ultimately thwart it. The only issue left was their repentance and this was what Joseph was after all along. This is why he did not reveal himself to them right away. Neither did he prematurely announce that he had forgiven them. Joseph's treatment of his brothers was therefore *active* in that Joseph moved *toward* his brothers; he did not passively "let go" of the hurt and move on with his life (which at this point was much better than ever before). His behavior was also in *their* best interest; that is, it was other-centered.

Joseph reassured his brothers not only with his words but also with his actions. He kissed all of them, wept over them, and talked with them for a long time. Although the brothers always suspected that one day Joseph would exact revenge, for the time being they were willing to enter into this new relationship with him. He had responded to their repentance with words of comfort. It is again important to emphasize that these words only came as a *response* to repentance, not as a unilateral offering to an unrepentant offender. And what were the words that Joseph used? They were certainly not what we might expect as words of forgiveness. He said, "Fear not" and "God is sovereign."

CHAPTER 9

DEFINING FORGIVENESS

Do not be afraid, for am I in God's place? As for you, you meant evil against me, but God meant it for good.
—Genesis 50:19–20

I n light of Joseph's response, this may be the right place to begin to construct a definition of forgiveness. Considering all I have said so far, it is obvious that there is no simple sound bite definition. Part of the problem is that true forgiveness can only occur in a specific context. To define it outside of that context turns it into something else. But even in its proper context, the substance of forgiveness can be confusing.

The context of forgiveness consists of two pre-existing conditions. First, there has to be repentance on the part of the offender and second, there has to be a substantial amount of healing on the part of the victim. These two conditions need to be in place before forgiveness can occur. Thus they are not the same as forgiveness nor do they produce forgiveness on their own. Rather, they set the stage for forgiveness. Repentance will be discussed in the next chapter, but here I want to emphasize that true forgiveness can only occur when the victim has experienced substantial healing.* Following

---

* In this section, I am referring to a case in which trauma has occurred. Obviously, in the case of day-to-day sin, the process can be accelerated.

God's example (who is eternally intact), the victim must approach any attempt at forgiveness from a position of strength or health. God does not forgive to be healed of anything. He does not forgive unilaterally in order to avoid physical and emotional symptoms. In fact, Scripture shows over and over again that God forgives *for the sake of the offender*, that is, His forgiveness is *other-centered*. Furthermore, He does not seek to lower His blood pressure by passively accepting that sin happens. Instead, He actively pursues those who have sinned in order that He may forgive them. So His forgiveness is active, not passive.

THE ROLE OF HEALING

Thus, if healing is a prerequisite to forgiveness, what constitutes healing? I would suggest first that if a victim is going to actually reengage an offender, the victim must first have achieved some sense of safety, that is, a belief and assurance that the offender can no longer hurt her. At a basic level, this safety would require physical security. Physical security may include but not be limited to establishing boundaries, limiting contact, moving to a safe environment, restraining orders, police protection, or even individual personal steps such as taking a self-defense class or buying and learning how to use a gun.

While establishing physical safety can reasonably protect against further physical damage, it is perhaps the emotional damage to which the victim remains most vulnerable, and which is harder to repair. As mentioned earlier, persistent nonrepentance effectively sustains the damage of the original trauma or offense. Add to this the fresh damage that can occur when a victim naïvely seeks to confront her perpetrator without taking proper protective measures. This is another reason why repentance is so important. Even with repentance, the response might be mixed, but without repentance, the victim is assured of a hostile response. Excuses, denial, and blame-shifting all serve to protect the offender at the expense of the victim. These defense mechanisms also attempt to challenge the victim's radar so as to shift the focus from the original offense to the victim's ability to see straight. If the victim is not prepared for this fresh attack, she can easily spiral back into a vortex of shame and self-contempt (which leaves the offender relatively unchallenged).

This is why confronting from a place of health is so important. If the victim has processed her own damaging cognitive reframes and learned to trust her own radar again, she is in a much stronger position to face her offender. Now his words of justifying and blame-shifting merely roll off of her to no effect. His words are powerless to hurt her any more. Because she has new armor and her radar is back online, she is no longer vulnerable to his verbal assaults. She can effectively "turn the other cheek."

As important as both physical and emotional safety is, substantial healing involves much more than just living a life of self-protection. Even if the victim never has to face her offender again, she still has to process the injustice of the original act and the constant temptation to reinterpret the world in ways that only serve to damage her soul further. The fact that the offender appears to have gotten away with his sin still haunts (and damages) the victim unless and until the victim comes to some kind of faith that justice will one day be served. This is where the promise of Romans 12:19 provides great assurance and comfort: "*'Vengeance is mine; I will repay,'* says the Lord" (emphasis added). This is the validation by the higher Judge spoken of in Chapter 5. Believing that God will one day execute justice takes the burden of understanding it all now off of the victim's shoulders. Now the victim knows that her offender's reprieve is only temporary, and with that knowledge she can entrust justice to God and refocus her energy into her own health.

This is also where praying through the imprecatory psalms mentioned in Chapters 6 and 7 can play a key role. Crying out for justice to the all-powerful God of the universe who sees everything and keeps score can be of great comfort to the victim. Knowing that God hates sin more than anyone, emboldens the victim to pray that God would render a just verdict in her case. This includes pleading with God to specifically judge her offender.

Finally, once protection is in place and future justice is assured, there slowly emerges a desire for the offender to repent. This is often a significant turning point in healing as the victim shifts from an exclusive preoccupation with her own healing to a desire for the offender's healing, via repentance and forgiveness.

Closing in on a Definition

Assuming everything else is in place (repentance, safety, healing, etc.), there still remains the definition of forgiveness. What does it really mean when someone says "I forgive you"? When I teach this material in class, I often challenge the students to come up with a synonym for the word "forgive" in the statement "I forgive you." This exercise is usually more difficult than the students expect. They are often better at defining what it does *not* mean, such as denial, cheap grace, naïve restoration of relationship, and so on; but when pressed, they have difficulty constructing a positive definition of the word. Often because of the popularity of the unilateral forgiveness view, the best they can come up with is some version of "let it go."

NO LONGER NEED TO FEAR

If we return to the story of Joseph, I believe we get a good clue as to what is involved in genuine forgiveness. Joseph's words to his brothers in Genesis 50 reveal what is often the primary need of those who seek to be forgiven. They need the fear of punishment to go away. Once an offender is finally struck with what he did and the response it deserves, there is often, along with repentance, a sense of grief, self-contempt, and fear. He knows that he has charged up a debt to his victim (and God) that he cannot realistically pay off. Grief comes from knowing he made a wrong decision. Self-contempt often follows when he sees his offense for what it was and stops defending himself. In light of what he did there is a subsequent revulsion with his very person. He begins to wonder how he could ever commit such an offense, and what it says about him. Finally, there is the fear that he will be exposed, judged, and sentenced. Initially this fear relates to the victim but ultimately, the offender is afraid of the court trial in which the victim will only be a witness. It is the judge who will eventually pass sentence and this is something to genuinely be afraid of if the offender is guilty. This is what the victim has been praying for all along (through language similar to that in the imprecatory psalms). In response to all of these fears, Joseph says to his brothers, "Fear not" (v. 19). Joseph's primary goal in this discussion was clearly directed toward reassuring his brothers that, once and for all, their fears were no longer necessary.

Several stories from Jesus's life reinforce this idea that part of genuine forgiveness is to consider the emotional state of the repentant offender. During one of His first preaching and healing ministries around the Sea of Galilee, Jesus was presented with a man who is described as a paralytic (Matt. 9:1–7; Mark 2:3–12). While it is not exactly clear what this man was suffering from, it is obvious that he could not even move, as his friends were required to get him anywhere close to Jesus. But when Jesus met him, He did not immediately heal him. Instead He said to the man, in effect, "Cheer up, your sins are forgiven." Apparently in this case, Jesus thought the man's need for forgiveness was much more pressing than his need to be healed. Thus, He granted him forgiveness. But this forgiveness was prefaced by the encouraging imperative, "Cheer up." If the man still could not walk at this time, what was there to cheer up about? Apparently, Jesus could see that this man had a deeper fear than never walking again.

Similarly, when a woman whom everyone recognized as a "sinner" (Luke 7:37) came to Jesus and assumed the role of a servant (an indication of her repentance) by anointing His feet with perfume and her tears, Jesus did not recoil but rather blessed her with two wonderful promises. After exposing the nonrepentance of the other sinners at the table (vv. 40–47), Jesus turned to the woman and said, "Your sins have been forgiven" (v. 48). The verb is a perfect passive in Greek and could be translated, "Your sins stand forgiven and this forgiveness will continue to have an ongoing impact on you." This was great news for the woman. The huge debt she had racked up (and could never pay off in several lifetimes) was all paid in full. After the other sinners (who were still in debt) interrupted Jesus with a challenge to His identity (v. 49), Jesus blessed the woman again with the statement that it was her faith that saved her (v. 50). Because she could never pay off her debt, this was also wonderful news. Any new debt she would accrue would also be paid off, not by her or anything she could do, but rather by Christ and what He was about to do and her faith in His work. Based on these two promises, Jesus could indeed encourage the woman to "go in peace," that is, live her life in light of the fact that her debt was forever paid. Like Joseph's brothers before her, she had no more reason to fear.

Even during His painful crucifixion, Jesus found an opportunity to share good news with a sinner. When Jesus was placed between the two thieves, they at first joined in with the verbal abuse hurled on Him by the bystanders (Matt. 27:44; Mark 15:32). However, something amazing happened in just a relatively short time. One of the thieves recognized that only two of them were paying the price for their sin that day. The One in the middle was not paying for anything He had done. There was something special about Him. The thief began to suspect that the One to whom he owed the largest debt might actually be paying it off right in front of him. The sign above this special Man was true. He was a king. Knowing his own life was coming to an end (and thus he would have no opportunity to do anything about his debt), the thief threw himself on the mercy of this King. Jesus's reply echoes the comfort that Joseph extended to his brothers. Jesus in effect said, "Fear not" when He promised that shortly they would be together in paradise even though the thief could never pay the entrance fee.

What was the basis for Jesus's call for these sinners to "cheer up"? They still warranted a death sentence for their sin but Christ was going to pay that price *for* them. They were no longer obligated to pay, as their debt would be paid in full, permanently. Jesus Himself was about to be the payment. Justice was not thrown out here. Good news indeed.

God Is Sovereign

The next phrase uttered by Joseph after "Fear not" was, "Am I in God's place?" (Gen. 50:19). What was behind this phrase and why would Joseph try to comfort his brothers by saying it? Joseph realized that all sin involves not only running up a debt with the victim but also running up a debt with God (see treatment of Psalm 51 in the next chapter). Ultimately, then, God is the final Judge and the final One to execute the sentence. Because God is the highest judge, His verdict is final. Thus if God pronounces someone forgiven, His judgment trumps all others. I believe Joseph was recognizing that there are some situations in which God had deemed that forgiveness was appropriate and if this was one of them, Joseph would not go against God and refuse to forgive. As mentioned earlier, believers do not have the option of choosing Spring's first category, *unconditional unforgiveness*.

Recognizing God's ultimate authority also laid the groundwork for Joseph to remind his brothers of God's sovereignty and goodness, another integral part of forgiveness. "What you meant for evil against me, God meant for good" (Gen. 50:20). Even though sinful acts cannot be undone and require a price to be paid, those sinful acts are never the end of the story. God always gets to write the final page and the story will always end with His plan being carried out. This again is great news for the offender. No matter what he did, God was watching the whole time and will somehow redeem it into something good. For example, who would have ever believed that callously selling your little brother as a slave would one day result in that same brother rising to a position second only to Pharaoh and thus becoming the source of deliverance for the very ones who had sold him? Only God could have imagined such a fantastic plot twist because that was what He was planning all along. Something similar happened when God decided to forgive a zealous, murderous Pharisee and turn him into the chief apostle to the Gentiles. And in one of the greatest reversals in history, when the evil one thought he had finally killed the Redeemer, Jesus rose from the dead and in doing so paved the way for all who believe to escape the evil one's grasp.

Many passages remind us of God's sovereignty and goodness. Even though Romans 8:28 (NIV) is misused at times, there is still the reassuring claim that "we know that in all things [even horrendous acts of evil], God works for the good those who love him, who have been called according to his purpose." And the Old Testament parallel, Jeremiah 29:11 (NIV), states, "'I know the plans that I have for you,' declares the LORD, 'plans to prosper you and not to harm you, plans to give you hope and a future.'" In spite of the fact that the recipients of this promise were currently in exile and had no prospect of going home, God still claimed He had "good" in store for them.

Ephesians 1:11 (NIV) reminds us that we are predestined "according to the plan of him who works out *everything* in conformity with the purpose of his will." Is there anything (especially sin) that occurs and wrecks irreversible damage *outside* of God's sovereign power and will? This verse seems to claim that there is no such category. This is great comfort, both to victims seeking some good to come out of what they suffered, and to sinners (all of us) when we realize that even our disastrous and evil choices cannot occur outside of God's control or capacity to redeem. His plans are still guaranteed and He is in control. This means that whatever happens, nothing and no one is beyond God's redemptive power. Understanding this about God contributes to the healing of both victim and offender. Since we are to model Jesus's forgiveness, we must embrace the truth that there is no sin or trauma that God cannot redeem.

The illustrations in Scripture of God's power to redeem evil are numerous. One vivid example is the metaphor of locusts used by the prophet Joel. In speaking of the last days, when God will have His final victory over sin, Joel provides a dramatic reminder of how God can bring life out of utter devastation. In ancient times there were few forces more thoroughly destructive than a swarm of locusts. They numbered in the millions and with several varieties, very little would survive their devouring (Joel 1:4). Their voracious appetite could turn a bountiful land into a desolate wilderness in a very short time, leaving nothing living in their wake (2:3). The people dependent upon the fruit of this land could easily conclude that nothing could recover from such a devastating attack, and yet God promised that even a locust attack could not thwart His ultimate plan to restore His people. The locusts were not the end of the story. God promised that one day, "I will repay you for the years the locusts have eaten. . . . You will have plenty to eat, until you are full, and you will praise the name of the LORD your God, who has worked wonders for you; never again will my people be shamed" (2:25–27, NIV). If God can restore the land after a locust attack, He can bring good out of the devastation that our sin incurs.

Some might conclude that death is at least one example in which evil's power is irreversible, and yet God demonstrates that not even death can escape His redemptive power. Another vivid example from the Old Testament is the sermon of Ezekiel about dry bones (Ezek. 37:3–6, NIV). Many commentators have recognized a prophetic element here but I would like to focus solely on the fact that God *can* and *does* bring life even out of death. God asks in verse 3, "Can these bones live?" Ezekiel must have suspected something was up and therefore he gave the correct theological answer: "Sovereign LORD, you alone know." What follows is a stunning demonstration of God's ultimate power. "This is what the Sovereign LORD says to these bones: I will make breath enter you, and you will come to life. I will attach tendons to you and make flesh come upon you and cover you with skin; I will put breath in you, and you will come to life. Then you will know that I am the LORD" (vv. 5–6). In the next seven verses, this phrase is repeated two more times, as if God wanted to make a clear statement as to just who was responsible for bringing life out of death. Even when the people said, "Our bones are dried up and our hope is gone; we are cut off" (i.e., sin has had the final word in our case), their words were overridden by God's: "'I am going to open your graves and bring you up from them; I will bring you back to the land of Israel. . . . Then you will know that I the LORD have spoken, and I have done it, declares the Lord" (vv. 12, 14, NIV). Even death cannot thwart God's redemptive power. Of course, the final victor over death is the One who claimed, "I am the resurrection and the life; he who believes in Me *will live even if he dies*" (John 11:25, emphasis added).

Not only does God prevail over sin in the life of an individual, but one day He will defeat sin everywhere. All the damage will be reversed and the God of sovereign goodness will reign forever (Rev. 22:1–5). In the words of Joseph, what was ultimately meant for evil (the seduction and fall of the human race by the evil one), God will one day work out permanently for good. Thus, no matter what, God wins in the end.

Toward a Final Definition

So what are we left with in our attempt to define forgiveness? What is my answer to the question that I ask my students? What does "I forgive you" really mean? What I have said up to this point is that human forgiveness needs to be modeled after God's forgiveness, requires repentance, is other-centered, and is active. It also presupposes a level of healing or intactness on the part of the victim. All of this can take time in many cases but, apart from a resolute position of unconditional unforgiveness (an option not available to a believer), eventually there will be the opportunity to offer genuine forgiveness. Perhaps part of what is being offered is recognition of the reversal of Murphy's levels of damage mentioned earlier. First, through His healing, God takes care of the damage of the original sin. Then, the offender's repentance stops the hostile messages of nonrepentance, setting the stage for the victim to feel less pressure to cognitively reframe the sin away. Finally, in light of this process, the relationship between the offender and the victim changes, hopefully in a healthy direction. To put it all in one comprehensive statement, my full exposition of "I forgive you" might go as follows:

> *Because of your repentance and the facts that the price for your sin has been paid (by God), the effects of your sin against me have been substantially healed, and your repentance has stopped the previously hostile messages to me, your sin can no longer damage me. Since you are taking responsibility for your sin, I no longer have to make up distorted reasons why it happened, and that is good for both of us. Finally, our relationship is now different and I agree to treat you in light of this new relationship.*

A Word about How Forgiveness Changes Relationships

The last part of this definition involves a change in relationship between offender and victim. Care must be taken when identifying the nature of this change. Many might assume that this change represents nothing more than resuming the relationship as it was before the betrayal. For example, imagine a married couple who separate due to unfaithfulness on the part of one or both parties. If repentance is offered and forgiveness granted, most would assume the couple could resume living together and pick up where they left off before the betrayal. But I wonder if this can ever really happen. Yes, they can move back in together, but can the relationship ever be *exactly* as it was before the betrayal? Trusting someone who has never betrayed me is risky enough; trusting someone who has already betrayed me is an even larger risk. Whether there is a season of counseling, initiation and implementation of church discipline, or even just an increased vigilance, these changes characterize a relationship that was *not* present before trust was violated.

Likewise, someone who is suspended from ministry due to a moral failure should not *demand* that relationship change mean a reinstatement to ministry. Nor should a perpetrator of sexual trauma *require* that his victim treat him as if no betrayal has occurred. Often the offender is so preoccupied with recovering his former relationship, that he is blind to the fact that what he had before was based at least partly on trust; when that trust is violated, the relationship as he remembers it is no longer possible. For an offender to demand that a relationship based on trust be resumed when trust has been betrayed would call into question the authenticity of the repentance being offered (see the next chapter for more on authentic repentance).

So if the change in relationship is not a return to the previous relationship, what kind of relationship is it? Just because the original relationship can never be resumed, as if no betrayal took place, does not mean that the relationship between offender and victim cannot change at all for the better. Indeed it should change. While the previous relationship based on trust is a thing of the past, the subsequent relationship based on untrustworthiness, betrayal, and nonrepentance is also a thing of the past (pending authentic repentance and forgiveness). Therefore, if the original relationship of trust is impossible, and the guarded relationship based on nonrepentance is no longer relevant, I believe some kind of *new* relationship needs to be established between victim and offender that somehow reflects that they now both agree on what happened. They both agree that sin occurred and that it should not have. They also both agree that the offender's repentance is authentic enough to warrant a reevaluation of the relationship. Even as they attempt to build this new relationship, some characteristics of the old, guarded relationship (before repentance and forgiveness) probably need to be retained.

For example, no church would responsibly allow a convicted sex offender to volunteer in its children's ministries. Most would assume the rationale for this policy is to protect the kids. While this is true, the policy also benefits the sex offender, for it removes him from an environment of enticement for which he experiences a pull that he has proven is difficult to resist. For a sex offender, temptation should not distract from worship. Thus it is good for the church, *and for him,* to limit his ministry to that which does not involve children.

Likewise, there may need to be some permanent boundaries in the future relationship between victim and offender, even if genuine repentance and forgiveness have occurred. Each case is unique and the boundaries may look different depending on the situation. But two extremes must be avoided—unconditional unforgiveness on one hand, and naïvely trying to resume what was lost on the other.

In some cases it may be best for there to be no ongoing relationship between offender and victim. There may have been no relationship in the first place (i.e., stranger rape), but any kind of personal relationship might provoke unnecessary interference with growth in both of their lives. Again, neither one *needs* a relationship in order to move forward. Some relationships may have to wait until heaven. I imagine in heaven that the martyr Stephen and the apostle Paul (who never had a chance to be forgiven by Stephen) have a much better relationship there than they ever had on earth.

Even if there is no ongoing interaction between victim and offender, one way the relationship could change is how the victim modifies her prayers for her offender. Prior to repentance, her prayer would appropriately include cries for justice (see the imprecatory psalms) and prayers that the offender would experience a change of heart (i.e., repent). But now, after repentance and forgiveness, her prayers can shift to petitioning God to strengthen the offender as he strives to live out his new life based on repentance.

CHAPTER 10

AUTHENTIC REPENTANCE

Be on your guard! If your brother sins, rebuke him; and if he repents, forgive him. And if he sins against you seven times a day, and returns to you seven times saying, "I repent," forgive him.

—Luke 17:3–4

Most of this book has attempted to take issue with the inadequate definitions given in the forgiveness literature in the context of an offender's nonrepentance. When the perpetrator will not admit that he was wrong, it puts the victim in a dilemma. In such cases, the question becomes: Must forgiveness be redefined, or can it be postponed? I have tried to make the case that postponing forgiveness is a much better option than redefining it in such cases. But what if the condition for forgiveness is met and repentance is offered? Most would say that forgiveness is much easier to grant in such cases, but does repentance make forgiveness any easier to define? Spring, whose work has been previously discussed here, considers it much easier. This is what she refers to as genuine forgiveness, in which the offender authentically repents and the victim authentically forgives.

However, even in these situations, it is often not as clear-cut as it appears. For if the offender is claiming to repent, the emphasis shifts from defining and recognizing forgiveness to defining and recognizing true repentance. When an offender verbalizes his recognition of wrongdoing, does that completely resolve the issue or only begin to resolve it? Following a statement of repentance, the victim then has to make some kind of evaluative judgment as to whether repentance has really occurred or not in order to really forgive. Depending on how long this takes, forgiveness could still be postponed.

The next problem becomes defining true repentance. This is an important issue, especially if repentance is required for forgiveness. If there is such a construct as true repentance, there must also be versions of counterfeit repentance. And if repentance can be faked, can the victim ever afford to trust that something real has happened in the heart of the offender? It is impossible to be absolutely clear, but it seems that true repentance involves both words and actions, and that forgiveness is most authentic when it is granted in the context of preexisting healing.*

Authenticating Repentance with Words

Words carry great power, so much so that the author of Proverbs declares, "Death and life are in the power of the tongue" (18:21). If words have such impact, what are the words required that constitute repentance? It seems pretty clear from Scripture that the qualifying statement is some version of "I was wrong." First John 1:9 identifies confession (words stating that we agree with God's assessment that we are guilty) as the prerequisite to forgiveness for our sins. Matthew 18:15ff is the well-known passage instructing those who have been victimized to go to their offenders and confront them with the hope that the offender will "listen," that is, vocalize agreement with the victims. This listening is enough to satisfy the requirements and no further action is needed. Most conversations between believers should go this way. It is only when the offender will not listen (i.e., agree and repent) that further action is required. "I was wrong" is such a simple statement but it is so easily diluted or weighed down with superfluous contingencies. This may be

---

* Again, this process can be accelerated by instant repentance. In such cases the victim does not have to endure the tension of disagreeing with her offender and thus is relieved of the task of constructing an explanation for what happened. They both agree from the beginning that what was done was wrong. I think this is the natural rhythm that Jesus is aiming for when he says that repentance warrants forgiveness even if it is several times in the same day.

part of the reason that God led David to express his repentance so clearly in writing Psalm 51.

David was a "man after God's own heart," yet he was far from perfect. Having a passion for God did not stop David from sinning, but I believe it did soften his heart so that when Nathan confronted and identified him—"You are the man!" (2 Sam. 12:7)—David replied with only the simple admission "I have sinned against the LORD" (v. 13). No excuses, no rationalizations, no listing of extenuating circumstances—just a simple statement, "I was wrong." However, behind these words was a depth of emotion that David gave vent to when he wrote Psalm 51.

The first obvious characteristic of this psalm is that David is not excusing himself. He knows he is guilty and he is therefore casting himself on God's mercy. Second, David blames no one but himself. He does not blame his loneliness, his midlife crisis, or Bathsheba's irresistible sex appeal for his sin with her. As for his authorizing the murder of Uriah, Bathsheba's husband, David could have justified it as the best of several bad options, but he does not. (A common excuse given by some Christian leaders caught trying to cover up for some moral failure is that exposure might jeopardize the continued success of the ministry). Nor does he blame his fear of exposure once he realized that Bathsheba was pregnant with his child. The only hint of a reason for his behavior is the admission that he was born in sin, but this is a universal variable and does not serve as an excuse for why any particular person sins in a particular way. Third, David realizes that the main one he has sinned against is God. He only hints at his sin of having Uriah murdered and does not mention his sin with Bathsheba at all. It is clear that murder and adultery are sins against other human beings but all sin is against God, who established those prohibitions in the first place. David concludes his psalm with the humble recognition that even though he was one of the most powerful monarchs of his time, there was nothing he could do to erase the sins he had committed. All he could do was throw himself on the mercy of God, who required no external payment but rather an internal brokenness (vv. 16–17).

In contrast to David's simple (albeit very difficult) admission of his sin, there are several scriptural examples of words that sound like repentance but upon careful examination reveal something other than repentance emerging from the heart. All such attempts serve to dilute rather than validate repentance. One common example is to offer repentance as a pain reliever. It is as if God is twisting someone's arm and he gets tired of the agony and so he cries "uncle" or some other word of capitulation. Sadly, this is probably the type of repentance practiced by the nation of Israel both before and after the kingdom was divided. Consider the high-sounding repentance speech given in Hosea 6:1–2 (NIV):

> Come, let us return to the Lord.
> He has torn us to pieces
>   but he will heal us;
> he has injured us
>   but he will bind up our wounds.
> After two days he will revive us;
>   on the third day he will restore us,
>   that we may live in his presence.

At first glance this appears to be an attempt to reconcile with God, but what is missing is the clear statement of wrongdoing characteristic of David in Psalm 51. Notice that the emphasis in this passage seems to be on the pain suffered *by the sinner* rather than on the sin that was committed. There is a recognition that God has caused pain but the ultimate theme seems to be that God (presumably after He calms down from His anger) will once again see their pain and bind up their wounds and in a few days everything will be fine again. There is no mention of what brought on the pain (their sin) in the first place. As gripping as a story of bringing pain to God might be, it is not a story of repentance. Focusing on the pain sin brings to the perpetrator rather than on the sin itself is just more self-absorption and deception. It is the pain suffered by the victim that should be the central point of repentance, not the pain suffered by the perpetrator incurred by his own sin.

Another way to counterfeit repentance is to distract by means of strong emotional display. How often have we seen famous people shed copious tears as they stutter out their regret of their behavior? On the surface it appears their hearts are broken over their sin (at least that is the most common interpretation for strong emotional displays) and we assume that such emotion must come from somewhere authentic. But tears are often disarming and at least initially invite the observer to extend sympathy rather than objective analysis. When we observe someone who appears to be in deep emotional pain, it seems to add an authenticity to his words that we might not otherwise grant were we to evaluate his words based on their content alone. Of course God is never deceived by such emotional displays, which qualifies Him to critique the "repenters" in Hosea 7:14 with the following: "They do not cry to Me from their heart when they wail on their beds." Thus crying and even wailing do not by themselves constitute nor validate repentance. Rationalization is another form of faux repentance.

A very common pattern of partial and postponed repentance is illustrated in the story of King Saul refusing to obey God when told to totally annihilate the Amalekites and all their possessions (1 Sam. 15). When first confronted by Samuel, Saul had the audacity to claim that he had actually obeyed the Lord (v. 13). When the sheep, which were supposedly dead, started bleating, Saul had to modify his position. His amended claim was that some of the spoils were reserved for sacrifices (v. 15). When this did not satisfy Samuel, Saul proceeded to blame the people (vv. 21, 24). Saul did claim to recognize that he had done wrong but he always added something to his repentance that justified why what he did was not so bad. He engaged in a time-honored subterfuge of saying, "I am sorry, but. . . ." Everyone knows that whatever comes after the "but" is what the person really means, and that what occurs before the "but" is just a setup. There is a clear difference between "I know I should not have talked to you that way *but* I had a hard day" and "I had a hard day *but* I still should not have talked to you that way. The qualification reveals the speaker's true intention.

In the case of Saul, his apology or repentance follows this deceitful pattern. He is effectively saying, "I am sorry that I disobeyed but the people took matters into their own hands and I could not stop them." Even when Samuel gave him several chances to come clean, Saul still begged for some show of honor before the people. True repentance merely confesses; it does not negotiate.

Admitting we are wrong and not adding anything to it involves a great deal of emotional vulnerability. This is why these words are so difficult for most of us to pronounce. We do not repent naturally which is why it can feel strange when we do it. To cite a personal example: Many years ago, my family was living in Chicago during the year that the White Sox won the

World Series. Most of the city (some Cubs fans are hopeless) was excited and cheering on the home team. People would sneak out of work to check their radios, computers, or phones for the scores during the daytime play-off games. Fortunately for me, the class I was teaching ended before the end of the game and I was able to watch the last few exciting innings on my computer in my office. Unfortunately I forgot that we only had one car, and that I was expected to come home right away that day so my wife could take the car to the class she was teaching. As soon as the game was over, I rushed to my car and rushed out onto the interstate to begin my journey home. That was the last of the rushing that day—because I had waited so long to leave, I was now stuck in Chicago's famous rush-hour traffic. When I got home late, I knew I was wrong and I suspected that my wife would be (rightly) upset. I decided I would not try to offer any excuses but rather just say I was wrong and I was sorry (I genuinely was sorry, especially when I saw the hurt in her face). So I did. And a surprising thing happened. She kissed me and thanked me for admitting I was wrong. Then she turned to leave and said, "I forgive you." This incident was a lesson on the wonder and glory of being forgiven. But it also struck me how hard it was for me to admit I was wrong. I probably needed every minute of rush-hour traffic to muster up enough courage to do the right thing.

Of course for some people, words of repentance are not that difficult, because they are not real. Like any other words, words of repentance can be riddled with deception and guile. Just because someone states words of confession on the outside does not mean something important has happened on the inside. We have all witnessed the public figures (politicians and church leaders are the most common) who are caught in scandal recite their rehearsed "repentance speeches," sometimes even accompanied by public tears as mentioned earlier. It is so common, that it has almost become its own genre. In such cases, we want to believe that their contrition is authentic, but we are suspicious. Thus we need proof that their words are real.

Authenticating Repentance with Behavior

According to Spring, the burden of forgiveness stays with the guilty party until he has proven his repentance. Some Christians are uncomfortable about this approach of having to "earn" forgiveness, especially because there does not seem to be any such precedent in Scripture.

However, since it is possible that the offender is merely lying to retain the comfortable life that he is at risk of losing, there must be some criteria by which to assess true repentance. Words of repentance may seem easier to evaluate on the surface. But even when the words seem to be correct, the real proof is in the subsequent behavior following the repentance speech.

So what behaviors indicate repentance, or the lack thereof? Obviously, if the offender blatantly continues the sin for which he so garrulously repented, it would be a pretty clear indication that his repentance was fairly shallow. But often after a public repentance, there is a season when the offender does indeed cease from his sinful behavior (whether through fear, subterfuge, or genuine repentance remains to be seen). Is this enough? Or are there signs that this repentance is either superficial or temporary? Again, only God can accurately diagnose someone's heart, but there are several behaviors that indicate whether or not repentance is genuine.

Indicator #1—No Demands

First, real repentance requires nothing—not even forgiveness—from the victim. There is no pressure for the victim to do anything. This calls into question the apparently innocent request, "Please forgive me." As a marriage counselor, I have witnessed one partner suddenly stop rationalizing and justifying his or her sinful behavior and spontaneously apologize. However, the apology often ends with a request that the victim instantly forgive the offender. This simple request actually shifts the burden from the offender back to the victim, which ultimately short-circuits the repentance process. The victim may not be ready to forgive, or even to understand what forgiveness involves in this particular case.

The reason why nothing should be required of the victim is that confession should be primarily for the sake of the victim and not just for the offender to get something off of his chest or feel absolved by a forgiveness statement by the victim. Understandably, when conviction of sin is working its way through someone's heart, there emerges a desire to confess with the expectation of some relief from the conviction. But this relief is God's responsibility, not that of the victim. Like David, the one we have most offended is God and confession should start there. After repenting to God, a desire and willingness to repent to the victim should naturally follow. But part of this confession is recognizing the impact that a confession might have on the victim. Usually, confession is a real gift to the victim. First, it stops the pain that comes from continuing nonrepentance. The victim no longer has to endure the damaging rationalizations and justifications for what was done to her. She and the offender finally see the situation the same way. Second, this in turn renders obsolete the victim's need to reconstruct reality. The victim no longer has to cognitively reframe the situation to reconcile her feelings of betrayal with the offender's feelings of nonrepentance—now she can more easily focus on her own continued healing. This focus on the victim is why this process is sometimes labeled with the construct "making amends."

However, there are cases in which repenting to the victim or making amends may feel like a re-traumatization. For example, if many years have elapsed since the sin, the victim may have chosen any one of a number of ways to move on with her life. In some cases she may have faced the pain head on and experienced a substantial level of healing. Other victims may have banished the event out of their conscious awareness. Years or even decades may have elapsed. To recklessly reopen an old wound is *not* taking the victim into consideration. Whatever the case, the offender does not have the right to unilaterally and arbitrarily barge into the victim's life, even to repent. In sum, a longing to confess is a good sign; a demand to confess (and/or be forgiven) is not.

Indication #2—Willingness to Assume Responsibility

If the offender really grasps that he is responsible for the sin, there should be a willingness and attempt to fix or clean up the mess that he has made. While the damage can never totally be eradicated, there needs to be a recognition that severe damage has been done and that a journey of healing is ahead. If the offender sees this, he will do what he can to facilitate that journey rather than hinder it. Maybe the victim needs time away from the offender to process what happened. The offender needs to be willing to give that time. This may involve something as drastic as attending a different church for a while to let the victim avail herself of the spiritual and emotional support that she is familiar with. As a very practical matter, the offender could offer to pay for counseling. In some cases the victim may want nothing from the offender. and that request needs to be honored also. Each case will be different but the common thread is a heart that is willing to help with the cleanup in whatever way possible.

Indication #3—Willingness to Pay Off the Debt over Time

This cleanup is not just a one-time event. There needs to be a willingness to continue to pay off the debt. For example, in the case of adultery, there is a loss of trust and the only way the offender can earn that trust back is by daily showing himself or herself trustworthy for a long time. Almost everyone finds paying off a debt as irksome, but the payments still have to be made. As of this writing, I am still paying off my school loan (however, the situation may change if this book sells well). I resent the money taken out of my account every month, just as it has been taken out for the last fifteen years. And yet I chose to incur that debt in order to get my doctorate, which was required for me to teach. I needed to borrow that money or I never would have been able to afford my degree. So I grudgingly admit that it was worth it and continue to pay off the debt. Admittedly, choosing to go to graduate school is a much healthier choice than choosing adultery, but in each case a debt was incurred that now needs to be paid off. It is understandable if the offender gets tired of paying back the debt, but if that ever becomes his main preoccupation over and above paying the debt for the sake of the victim's pain, his repentance has ceased to be genuine.

Finally, the offender can pray for the victim's healing (whether this leads to forgiveness or not). Regardless of any action or nonaction on the part of the offender, it is God alone who can eventually bring about healing. Praying for the victim on a regular basis reveals a heart that is primarily concerned with the healing of the victim rather than the self-centered preoccupation with mere catharsis. Consequently, this prayer for the victim's healing requires no updates from or contact with the victim.

ROLE OF PREEXISTING HEALING

Evaluating words and deeds to assess the level of repentance relates primarily to the offender. However, in order for repentance to have its greatest impact and lay the groundwork for genuine forgiveness, there needs to be a level of preexisting healing on the part of the victim. In other words, the victim needs to be in a place where she is ready (and able) to forgive.

Healing has already been addressed in several chapters of this book. It primarily involves appealing to God for justice (albeit sometimes delayed) and trusting that His verdict will be fair. Given that reassurance, the victim can more effectively dismantle the harmful cognitive reframes constructed to make sense of what happened. Furthermore, the victim's focus begins to shift from the intensity of her pain (which God is ultimately responsible to heal) to an other-centered concern for the offender and his repentance. However, sometimes the journey is long and involves many steps. Wisdom must be applied to locate where the victim is on the path. Premature forgiveness risks becoming cheap forgiveness if the victim has not properly processed what happened.

The offender should always be ready to confess and repent, but the victim may not be ready to forgive. Consequently, when the offender wants to postpone repentance it is usually a bad sign, but it is not necessarily a bad sign if the victim wants to postpone forgiveness. The timing, therefore, depends more on the victim than the offender.

CHAPTER 11

RESULTS OF FORGIVENESS

Blessed is the one whose transgressions are forgiven.
—Psalm 32:1 (NIV)

I n the last chapter I explored what forgiveness might look like in response to the offender's repentance. What does a victim really mean and what is a victim offering when she says, "I forgive you"? Here I would like to explore what happens *as a result* of genuine forgiveness. To put it in the form of another question I ask my students, "What changes five minutes after genuine forgiveness is granted?"

The first logical question is whether anything really changes at all during forgiveness. For example, if forgiveness is just the recital of a prepared statement, we might rightly question the value of such a statement. If nothing really changes, it is reasonable to question whether anything really happened and thus question the overall value of any forgiveness ritual. If nothing changes, it is fair to say that forgiveness does not have much power or value. Most advocates for forgiveness believe, however, that forgiveness does change something.

If forgiveness does indeed change something, the next issue is to recognize the distinction in results between unilateral and bilateral forgiveness. Unilateral forgiveness is similar to a giant cognitive reframe with all of the benefits and drawbacks that come with that. Choosing to see a situation differently usually brings with it a different (i.e., more pleasant) emotional response. Forgiveness that somehow involves the offender, on the other hand, would result in a slightly different set of benefits. In this case there is potential for more of the damage to be reversed and possibly for the relationship between the victim and offender to change for the better. Regardless, there are at least three categories of benefits that usually are associated with forgiveness.

Benefits of Forgiveness for the Victim

The main selling point of the majority of forgiveness writing is that something desirable *does* happen at the moment of forgiveness, especially when forgiveness is unilateral. In almost all such cases, the forgiveness literature refers to the victim releasing or letting go of some kind of toxic emotion such as anger, rage, hatred, desire for revenge, etc. Put in the simplest terms, the previous bad feelings go away. There are at least two assumptions that undergird this view.

The first assumption is that the "bad feeling" that the victim is seeking to let go of is not just unpleasant, but pretty toxic. Most of the time, words like "hate," "rage," and "desire for revenge" are chosen to conceptualize what the victim is feeling but needs to release. Logically this would mean that in response to interpersonal sin, the victim is also guilty of her emotional response (anger, rage, desire for revenge) and unilateral forgiveness is merely code for the victim repenting of her own sin.

But I question if these negative terms always accurately capture what is going on in the heart of a victim. Admittedly, anyone can hold a grudge and comfort herself with fantasies of revenge and these feelings would obviously be problematical. However, there seems to be no room for *legitimate* resentment of evil or a *valid* longing for justice (Romans 12 and the imprecatory psalms). All strong feelings are labeled with pejorative language and thus need to be purged. But as we have seen, God Himself responds to sin with pretty strong emotions and yet feels no need to purge Himself of these feelings. So the assumption that the unpleasant feelings are the main problem to be solved (and thus emotional release is the main goal) needs to be revised.

The second assumption is that these benefits are available apart from any interaction with the offender whatsoever. Because the offender need not be involved, the change is therefore limited to the heart of the forgiver. The victim is merely choosing to view the situation differently than she had previously. But she still has to deal with both the fact that the offender remains unrepentant and the hostile messages that accompany this position. She also has to deconstruct all of the hurtful cognitive reframes that she herself adapted in her attempt to deal with what happened. Finally, all of the relational benefits of forgiveness are not available. Thus it seems that for forgiveness to be fully experienced, the offender has to be involved somehow.

These perceived benefits of unilateral forgiveness differ from the case in which the offender genuinely repents and the victim consequently offers forgiveness to a real live person face to face. The most obvious difference is that because confession, repentance, and forgiveness are bilateral (i.e., involve both the victim and the offender), there is agreement on what actually happened—as opposed to just one party cognitively restructuring the situation. Therefore, the victim no longer has to endure the hostile messages of nonrepentance that give rise to damaging cognitive reframes. She also can finally name and face what happened to her without any contradictory explanations. This begins to revalidate her "radar," which in turn begins to reduce the need for an eternally vigilant, guarded lifestyle. Whenever and to whatever degree the offender admits blame, it takes a huge load off of the shoulders of the victim and can in many cases accelerate the victim's healing process.

BENEFITS OF FORGIVENESS FOR THE OFFENDER

While the primary motive for confession and repentance is for the sake of the victim, there are also great benefits to the offender; and just as with the benefits accrued by the victim, these benefits differ depending on the degree to which the victim is involved.

First, and most significant, is the experience of being forgiven by God. Whether the victim ever arrives at a place where she can formally forgive her offender, ultimately it is God that provides the basis for any forgiveness as He is the only one that can pay the enormous price for sin—it is too high for anyone else to pay, including the victim. The fact remains that "without shedding of blood there is no forgiveness" (Heb. 9:22) *for anybody*. However, even though the Old Testament sacrificial system foreshadowed this sacrifice, it was never meant to (nor could it) replace the ultimate sacrifice of Christ on the cross. It is only "the blood of Christ" that can "cleanse your conscience from dead works to serve the living God" (Heb. 9:11–14). Note both the objective and subjective cleansing here. The blood of Christ objectively wipes out the sin of the offender but it also subjectively helps the offender recognize and celebrate this cleansing. Not only does Christ's payment for sin impact the sin itself (by wiping it clean) but there is also an impact on the sinner's subjective analysis of his sin. In other words, God not only forgives sinners but He also helps them to *feel* forgiven.

In John Bunyan's classic work *The Pilgrim's Progress*, the author vividly describes the moment when Christian is freed of his heavy burden of sin:

> Now I saw in my dream that the highway up which Christian was to go was fenced in on either side with a wall, and that wall is called Salvation. Up this way therefore did burdened Christian run, but not without great difficulty, because of the load on his back. He ran thus till he came at a place somewhat ascending, and upon that place stood a cross, and a little below the bottom a sepulcher. So I saw in my dream that just as Christian came up with the cross, *his burden loosed* from off his shoulders, and fell from off his back and began to tumble, and so continued to do, till it came to the mouth of the sepulcher where it fell in and *I saw it no more*. Then was Christian *glad and lightsome* and said with *a merry heart*, "He hath given me rest by his sorrow and life by his death."[1]

The joy experienced by Christian was a direct result of his burden falling from his shoulders and into the abyss of Christ's death, burial, and resurrection. Bunyan wrote more than three hundred years ago, but celebrating God's forgiveness is a timeless privilege. Two contemporary Christian songs capture the objective and subjective glory of God's forgiveness. The first song, by Casting Crowns, is roughly based on the biblical promise found is Psalm 103:12, where the author celebrates that God has removed the sin of His people as far as the east is from the west.[2]

Resting in the arms of God's mercy is a wonderful subjective experience, but only if our sin is objectively banished so far away that we will never see it again. The main chorus of the second song, by Mercy Me, proclaims over and over again the objective statement that "the cross has made you flawless." In light of this glorious fact, the song goes on to encourage us to really *feel* what it is like to experience the truth of God's forgiveness.[3]

If the forgiveness of God is really this glorious and genuinely this real, forgiven sinners can indeed smile and tell ourselves that we are OK because the cross was truly enough. This is why the forensic view of forgiveness mentioned in Chapter 1 must *always* be the foundation for whatever else forgiveness means. The price for sin must be paid and the fact it has been paid is good news to sinners everywhere. In addition to paying the forensic price for sin, God also is always *ready* to forgive (Ps. 86:5) in response to repentance (2 Peter 3:9). He has no need to heal or deal with corrosive anger.

Part of the reason that God's forgiveness is so primary is that He is the primary *victim* of all sin regardless of any secondary victims. David confessed "against you and you alone have I sinned and done this evil in your sight" (Ps. 51:4). Anyone who knows the story of David's sin might understandably want to add Uriah (murder) and Bathsheba (adultery) to David's list of victims. Whatever David may have said or done to make things right with Bathsheba, in this his main psalm of confession, he seems more concerned with making things right with God. He knows better than to offer an elaborate sacrifice (v. 16). Maybe he already suspects the insufficiency of such an offering. Rather he just confesses his sin and throws himself on the mercy of the God he has wronged. David also looks forward to the subjective results of being forgiven when he asks God to "restore to me the joy of my salvation" (v. 12). Experiencing God's forgiveness is both necessary and sufficient for the offender to be forgiven and to feel forgiven. Not only is there relief from hiding but there is also relief from what was being hidden—that is, the offender's sin. This is the most significant change from the perspective of the offender.

However, there is an additional blessing if the offender is forgiven by his human victim. If the victim offers forgiveness in response to repentance, the offender gets a face-to-face taste of what it is like to be forgiven by God. The offender also receives the gifts that Joseph offered his brothers (Gen. 50:19–21). He no longer has to fear and he can live with confidence that God is overseeing everything and will somehow bring everything into compliance with His good will. The evil one will be defeated.

For all the benefits of the forensic aspects of forgiveness incurred by the offender, there is at least one benefit to the victim—her sins are paid for. I want to clarify that by claiming that the sins of both offender and victim are forgiven, I am not advocating moral equivalency. It is the offender's sin that bears the brunt of the burden of responsibility. However, as mentioned before, in response to the sin and the continued nonrepentance of the offender, the victim is often tempted to utilize destructive cognitive reframes that only perpetuate the damage to her soul. Here the victim becomes her own abuser as these cognitive reframes usually involve some version of blaming herself. Thus, the victim is offered forgiveness, not for something she did to the offender but rather something she has done to herself.

BENEFITS TO THE RELATIONSHIP
BETWEEN VICTIM AND OFFENDER

Finally, true repentance and forgiveness lay the groundwork for a change in the relationship between offender and victim. In the first chapter, I took issue with Shults and Sandage, who seemed to elevate relational forgiveness at the expense of forensic forgiveness. While they recognize that forensic forgiveness is mentioned in Scripture, they claim that Scripture paints forgiveness as much more relational in its fullest expression, rather than merely a forensic payment of a debt. I argued that without forensic forgiveness, there can be no relational forgiveness. There is a price to be paid, and without that payment there is no basis for any change in the relationship between offender and victim. Yet, I agree with Shults and Sandage that forensic forgiveness, while primary, is not exhaustive. There is a relational component to forgiveness and therefore true forgiveness must involve a change in relationship between victim and offender.

There are actually two relational changes that occur between offender and victim during the sin, repentance, and forgiveness process. First, there is a shift as a result of the sin. Whatever relationship that existed between victim and offender (who, prior to the sin, would not even relate to one another in these terms) changes when the sin occurs. This is when the offender becomes the offender and the victim becomes the victim. Prior to this, the two people could have experienced a wide range of relationship with each other, all the way from close intimate friends (including spouse, parent, or child) to total strangers. Whatever the level of relationship, this relationship changes as a result of sin.

Relationships are always experiencing change for a variety of reasons. Life circumstances, physical distance, and forming of new relationships with others are some of the many reasons relationships are always in a state of flux. Thus they are dynamic rather than static. To choose a moment in a relationship and make that snapshot the definitive portrait of the entire scope of the relationship would not accurately capture the real relationship.

But when one party betrays or hurts the other, the relationship is damaged and requires a response from both parties. This response further modifies the relationship. The offender usually compounds the damage by refusing to instantly repent, which robs the relationship of a sense of safety and trust. Thus, until the offender repents, he is no longer safe and this affects how much he can be trusted going forward in the victim's perspective. Therefore, to maintain a protective posture toward the offender in this case is not a sign of defensiveness or unforgiveness on the part of the victim, but rather a logical response to the fact that the offender objectively is not safe.

It therefore becomes a *different* relationship. In a very real sense, the prior relationship based on trust has been irreversibly destroyed. Now either both parties can live life based on this new reality ("our previous safe relationship is no longer safe") or as a result of repentance and forgiveness they can forge a new relationship based on *rebuilt* trust and safety. Because it is a new relationship, a return to the old or previous relationship is impossible. Either the relationship is permanently fractured or it is rebuilt. Regardless, it can never go back to what it was.

For example, a couple who has never experienced marital unfaithfulness has a different level of safety and trust than the couple who has weathered the storm of infidelity. To follow the metaphor of a storm, in one case the original house has remained firm, while in the other case the original house has been destroyed and a second house has been rebuilt in its place. Even though repentance and forgiveness have occurred, there is one sense in which the trust can never be fully restored to the level it was prior to being broken.

So a relationship that previously enjoyed a level of trust, security, and faithfulness has changed in that it no longer provides these benefits. But this relationship can undergo further change as a result of forgiveness based on repentance. This is the second major relational change that occurs between victim and offender. Once again, the level of change depends a great deal on the involvement of both parties.

From a unilateral perspective, it is true that we can choose to behave however we like toward anyone regardless of preexisting relationship. We can independently choose to betray our friends or to be kind to our enemies. In this sense, changing a relationship does not require both parties' cooperation. However, if the relationship is going to change *for the better*, as we presume it would as a result of forgiveness, there has to be at least some sense of a restoration of the trust and safety that has been lost. For this to occur, both parties have to play a role.

There are two extremes commonly put forth as possible positive changes in a relationship. On one extreme is the view that forgiveness, regardless of repentance, restores the relationship to the level of intimacy, trust, and safety that existed prior to the offense. It is similar to restoring a computer to a date and time before the virus infected the system. When this happens with a computer, it is almost as if the virus never happened (actually as I understand it, the virus is "quarantined" and thus can no longer harm the computer). Some believe that relationships work the same way. Repentance and forgiveness somehow restore a relationship *exactly* as it was before at a prior time.

While I believe a great deal of restoration can occur and married couples, for example, can rebuild after the storm of adultery, I still maintain that there is a difference between a faith that has been betrayed and one that has not. Even when God restored Adam and Eve, they still had to rebuild their life and relationship *outside* the garden. No matter how close Adam and Eve became after being banished from paradise, every time Adam pulled weeds in order to grow food or Eve experienced pain during childbirth, they would both be reminded that the relationship with God (and each other) was no longer as it once was.

If the trust of the original relationship has been destroyed, a demand by the offender to arbitrarily return to those days of faithfulness rather than apply effort to building something new that is based on the work of regaining trust should therefore be seen as a sign that his repentance is still in its infancy. Again, a demanding posture on the part of the offender is usually not a good sign. Some may cite the case of Hosea, who, under orders from God, buys back his wayward wife (Hos. 3:1–5). But is he nobler than another man who would file for divorce upon the grounds of unfaithfulness? It must be remembered that Hosea was acting under direct orders from God, not necessarily setting an eternal precedent for how spouses should respond when their mates are unfaithful.

The problem of restoring the relationship to a previous setting does not apply to situations where there is no preexisting relationship to which to return. Such is the case with anonymous rape or sexual assault. In such circumstances, it is sometimes seen as praiseworthy (and thus pressure is applied) for the victim to invite the offender to a new relationship where none existed before. But in my opinion, to pressure a victim to pursue such a relationship unfairly shifts the responsibility from the offender back to the victim again. In general, I believe the principle mentioned earlier: Anything that requires more vigilance on the part of the victim than that of the offender is probably not working toward real forgiveness.

If the offender had not wronged the victim in the first place, they might never have had any relationship of any kind and thus have no relationship to which to return. But now, because of the offender's sin, they do have at least a rudimentary relationship, that of offender and victim. Where does their relationship go from here? In one real sense, it is up to the victim. Consistent with the view that the offender should not exert pressure for restoration is also the view that the victim should be free to do what she feels is right in terms of what level of relationship, if any, she is willing to have. Some victims, for a myriad of reasons, may elect to correspond or visit their offenders in prison, offer forgiveness (usually unilaterally), and even offer to befriend their offenders when they are released. This type of posture toward an offender, while risky, is often seen as noble. But is this behavior nobler than the victim who chooses to have no further contact with her anonymous abuser? If she feels led to establish a relationship with her offender, it is her prerogative. But it is not required nor is it a sign of deeper forgiveness. Again, it needs to be emphasized that the victim should have the freedom to pursue whatever or wherever she feels God is calling her.

While the first extreme might be either to advocate for an unrevised return to a previous relationship, or to establish a relationship where none existed before, a second extreme is to conclude that repentance and forgiveness, while positive developments, really change *nothing* as far as the potential relationship between victim and offender. In this view sin has permanently destroyed whatever chance there might be for *any* kind of relationship, whether new or restored. Therefore victim and offender need not interact at all, and can both independently await the day when God makes all things new.

In one sense, this posture probably takes sin most seriously of all possible postures. However, taken to an extreme, this approach could easily morph into the "unconditional unforgiveness" option earlier identified by Spring and forbidden in the Bible. Whether we can fully explain it or not, God's forgiveness (the model we are trying to follow) always includes an element of joy at the resolution. God never forgives someone and then just walks away. He always throws a party (just like the father of the prodigal son). Because of God's effectual plan of salvation, He always turns His face *toward* those who have wronged Him rather than *away* from them. Something positive *always* comes of God's forgiveness, whether we ever see it or not. Remember, in his repentance speech in Psalm 51, David expected that when the process of repentance and forgiveness was all finished, God would restore his joy (vs. 12). We may not always be able to articulate how the relationship changes, but we must remain open to the fact that God can change any relationship for the better, according to His definition, which in some respects may remain a mystery. Even if the final relationship between victim and offender remains ambivalent and complex this side of heaven, there is no ambiguity about their relationship when they are both in the presence of Jesus at the end of time. On that day, there will be no more danger and thus no more fear or subsequent need for vigilance. The wolf (violent predator) will lay down with the lamb (innocent victim) forever (Isa. 11:6–10).

CHAPTER 12

FORGIVENESS AND JUSTICE IN COUNSELING

He is faithful and just and will forgive us our sin.
—1 John 1:9 (NIV)

T he distinction between theoretical understanding and practical application is often overblown. However, it is legitimate to ask that if all that has been said so far about forgiveness is true, what impact will that have on mentoring, pastoral care, and counseling? What about the case of Ellen and George and their assumptions about forgiveness? Should the counselor take a more active role and educate them about their confusion over forgiveness? Or should the counselor confront George about what appears to be his lack of genuine forgiveness? Maybe the counselor should start over and teach Ellen and George what forgiveness really means so they can truly forgive one another in a more authentic way.

APPLICATIONS TO COUNSELING

George and Ellen are not the exception when it comes to clients who are unclear about forgiveness. They probably reflect the norm. In fact, most clients enter therapy with some vague sense of what forgiveness means already in place, even though when pressed, they may not be able to provide an articulate or consistent definition. This is why they may use confusing and contradictory language such as, "I just need to forgive God" or "I just need to forgive myself." Regardless of their confusion about the nature of forgiveness, they are pretty clear on their vision of the results. Almost everyone believes that forgiving leads to feeling better (the marketing strategy for forgiveness has worked) and that is probably the unspoken or even unconscious goal of most clients who want help with forgiveness. Add to this the fact that most Christians believe it is their duty to forgive, whether they understand what it means or not, and there is a great deal of pressure to provide some kind of forgiveness formula and/or method. In light of this pressure, most clients come in with a favorable disposition and a receptive posture toward whatever the counselor might say as long, as it leads to appeasing God and feeling better.

This gift of trust can be tempting to a counselor. Knowing that the client wants to feel better fast and has temporarily put himself or herself at the counselor's disposal can trigger many issues for the counselor who is not self-aware. It can be a great feeling to produce for clients exactly what they ask for and for it to work (or at least work well enough), but this may or may not be what they really need. Naturally, when it does not work, this only makes things worse. Most clients cannot recognize that sometimes it is the therapist's treatment plan that is out of whack, not their own efforts or willingness to change. Of course the counselor always dodges the blame because we all know that "forgiveness is hard." But from the clients' perspective, if following the counselor's definition of forgiveness does not "work," the clients could easily blame themselves (they are pretty adept at this already) for being therapeutic failures.

Related to this is the power differential in the counseling setting. To the degree that the counselor strongly encourages the client to forgive (with or without a supplied definition), the issue can become one of therapeutic compliance rather than one of true forgiveness. The counselor's voice becomes even stronger in the case where the counselor already has a clean, ready-to-use definition of forgiveness and a step-by-step formula to follow. How could a client resist this? It could be very easy to confuse and substitute pleasing the counselor with the client's own personal work. Treatment compliance does not always indicate progress. For this reason, the first application for counselors is to not pressure the client into premature forgiveness.

Do Not Pressure Clients into Premature Forgiveness

What is premature forgiveness? It is forgiveness performed before the proper context (repentance and healing, as mentioned in Chapters 10–11) is in place or before any real understanding of forgiveness is achieved. Again, most clients will come in with some sense of what forgiveness means but because their unilateral efforts have not led to better feelings, they assume they are doing something wrong and want the counselor to tweak their forgiveness efforts so that they can feel much better. Two common complaints among clients are that forgiveness is either confusing and/or difficult.

In response to these complaints, the counselor could be tempted to insert his or her own favorite definition which, whether accurate or not, will probably be received favorably by the client due to the lack of any viable alternative. Working exclusively from the counselor's well-articulated step-by-step definition of forgiveness may provide structure to the sessions and measurable treatment goals, but leaves little space for the client to wrestle through the issue for herself. While this may reinforce the counselor's role as power broker, it does little to help the client to forgive.

Another way that a counselor can attempt to appease a client's anxiety is to apply moral pressure to the victim to forgive, usually in response to the offender's verbal apology. Strangely (and effectively from the offender's perspective), this apology often serves to switch the burden from the perpetrator, who needs to prove somehow that his heart is really repentant, to the victim who now has to prove that she has truly forgiven her offender. But if the only requirement for forgiveness is a verbal apology, this short-circuits the victim's ability to authentically think through what is really being offered in the name of forgiveness. For example, imagine a man caught in adultery and subjected to church discipline (after his wife has confronted him to no avail). When confronted by the elders and his wife, suppose he surprises everyone by instantly admitting he was wrong and requesting that his wife forgive him at that very moment. Understandably she would be taken off guard and desire time to process what had just happened before fully granting forgiveness. In response to her hesitancy, the husband could appeal to the elders to initiate church discipline *against her* for her unforgiving heart. Admittedly this is an extreme example, but if forgiveness is defined primarily as a moral or strictly legalistic imperative devoid of any internal or relational aspects, such a case is not that exaggerated.

A final danger in the counselor foisting his or her definition onto the client is that if the client is not fully persuaded (but is still treatment-compliant), there is a great risk that the forgiveness offered will merely be some form of cheap forgiveness mentioned earlier and thus not only postpone any real forgiveness but also invite further damage if she takes that definition with her when confronting her offender.

At this point, it might seem odd that I have written a whole book on improving the definition of forgiveness, and yet I am now advising counselors *not* to supply such a definition to their clients (at least not right away). But if the counselor does not provide a ready formula for forgiveness, what should he or she be doing? Rather than impose our definition of forgiveness (even if it is a good one), I believe it is more profitable at this stage to help the clients see that either they really do not have any real idea what forgiveness means, and/or the definition of forgiveness that they came in with is not well thought through. Again, most clients do not come to counseling to discuss and debate what forgiveness means. They want to feel better and they believe forgiveness is the means to that end. This desire to feel better (using forgiveness or anything else as a means) needs to be exposed. Does the client really want to forgive or does she just want the emotional pain to go away? The role of the counselor in this case is to help the client focus on forgiveness for its own value (not just as pain relief). This would often involve revisiting and wrestling with what forgiveness means in Scripture in all of its potential ambiguity. Thus, I think it is more authentic for clients to recognize for themselves that their superficial views of forgiveness are pretty foggy than for the counselor just to impose his or her view.

Validate the Longing for Justice

Rather than getting into a debate about the validity of anyone's definition of forgiveness, I think it is more beneficial to validate the client's pain and longing for justice. As mentioned before, most clients want to feel better so it is their painful feelings that need to be explored and validated, not minimized or critiqued. By postponing the discussion of forgiveness, the victim is free to look at what happened and the levels of damage that have rippled through her life as a result. Consider the following phrases as invitations for the client to embrace the painful feelings of her heart.

Something bad did happen to you. This statement addresses the first two levels of damage mentioned earlier. First, there is a recognition that sin really did occur. It was not a misunderstanding or an accident. There is no justification, rationalization, or excuse. It was wrong.

It should not have happened to you. This statement reinforces the evil of what was done and begins to challenge the client's propensity to cognitively reframe the situation into something that is a logical result of something she did or did not do. If something should not have happened, the client does not have to supply a legitimate reason why it did happen. It simply should not have happened.

It was not your fault. This statement is a logical outgrowth of the previous two phrases and probably needs to be said every session. One of the most common cognitive reframes in response to others' sin is to blame ourselves. While this reframe provides some sense of order to the world, in reality it only serves to re-traumatize the victim. I remember one couple trying to survive the sin of adultery. The wife was so disoriented by the sinful behavior of her husband that she was prescribed an antidepressant for a brief time. Since she was the only one taking medications, it was easy for her to conclude that she was the one whose thinking was distorted. In her mind, how could she rationally evaluate her husband's behavior when her judgment was so unreliable that she needed medication to think straight? Thus, she needed frequent reminders from me, as her counselor, that her assessments and appraisals were just as valid (even more so, in reality) as those of her husband. Very few medications can distort someone's thinking as severely as sin does. It was *his* thinking that was more distorted by sin than hers by medications. As a way to counter her fears, I required her to begin every session with the statement "I am not crazy." This provided at least some challenge to her natural inclination to blame herself. While at first this was seen as somewhat of a frivolous joke, eventually she started to believe what she was saying. In this case, her husband repented deeply, and soon he too was reassuring her that she was not crazy.

Your offender should face justice. If the offender is indeed guilty, he should face justice; and it is not unhealthy, dysfunctional, or wrong for the victim to pray accordingly. This is where the imprecatory psalms can be introduced, to provide language for the legitimate desire for justice. As mentioned earlier, our response to sin should be more than a cognitive recognition that sin has been committed. If evil has really occurred, there should be a longing for justice in the hearts of all who "love good and hate evil."

God will execute justice on his timetable. Once the victim embraces the truth that the offender deserves justice, there is an expectation that it will (or should) come swiftly. If God does indeed keep score, then why not settle the score now? We do not know the full reasons why God postpones justice. One reason is that He is waiting for more offenders to repent (2 Peter 3:8–9) but this does not explain why God chooses at times to bring judgment rather quickly (as in the case of Ananias and Sapphira, Acts 5) and at other times postpones it for many years (as in the case of Ahab and Jezebel, 1 Kings 16–2 Kings 9).

All of these phrases invite clients to explore the damage that was done to them without some external pressure to prematurely perform some forgiveness ritual. However, seeing the damage for what it is does lay the groundwork for what the Bible claims is the real essence and motive of forgiveness.

Shift from Focus on Victim to Focus on Offender

Feeling validated in personal pain is never the final step in the healing journey. As the client begins to grow, look for the shift from self-centeredness (concern over her own healing) to other-centeredness (concern for the perpetrator's healing). As the victim embraces her own pain and begins to heal, the direction of her heart and focus begins to shift outward instead of always inward. When the victim realizes that God really does keep score and that judgment is coming to the offender because she has turned justice over to God, she is then free to actually care about the offender and his future (or maybe pour coals of fire on his head?). This is when real empathy can serve a purpose (unlike that mentioned in Chapter 2). Facing divine judgment can be a scary proposition. A sinner in the hands of an angry God is not safe, and any logical person facing God's judgment should immediately repent and throw himself or herself on the mercy of the divine Judge. The client now sees this and is concerned that if the offender does not repent, God's justice is on its way.

Prepare for the Offender's Repentance

If the client is shifting to a more other-centered focus and is convinced that God's justice is on the way, there begins to emerge a genuine desire for the offender to repent, even though this might call for the client to actually think through what forgiveness might require of her. Without any repentance, the client can postpone forgiveness. But when repentance occurs, the client needs to at least explore how God might be calling her to forgive. Forgiveness as a response to repentance is still not an easy matter. Many victims prefer never to face their offenders again rather than have to assess and respond to repentance. Up until now, prayers involving the offender have been prayers for justice (i.e., imprecatory psalms). However, once the victim is convinced that the offender can no longer hurt her and that judgment really is coming, prayers for repentance are often added to prayers for judgment. Once again, the counselor does not pressure for this shift; rather it occurs as a regular part of the victim's healing. But praying that the offender might repent is a risky prayer because God might actually answer that prayer. Just ask Jonah.

Thus, part of therapy at this stage is to both pray and prepare for the day when the offender might actually repent. Praying for this day opens up a whole new vulnerable part in the heart of the client. Not only must she mentally accept that her offender *might* repent, but she also must recognize and embrace the part of her that *wants* him to repent. This desire is accompanied by a great deal of ambivalence. On one hand, if her offender remains unrepentant, little is required of her and she can maybe more easily move on with her life. However, she knows that if the victim genuinely repents, something might be required out of her in response.

> Sample prayer: "God, you know what happened to me and you know who did it. I trust you to see that justice is done. I know that if my offender does not repent, he will have to answer to you. Because of the concern you are growing in me for my offender, I would ask that you would convict him and lead him to repentance. Furthermore, if you want me to play a role in his repentance, I am willing to do that with your help."

Whenever we ask God for something, we are at least entertaining the possibility that He might grant our request. Thus, to pray that our offenders repent without preparing for that day calls into question our view of prayer. Practicing with a counselor can be of great help both in clarifying the issues in the victim's mind and also reducing some of the anxiety that might arise from a sudden confession from the offender. Specific strategies might include rehearsing, role-play, and trying out responses under the counselor's safety net. This preparation should lead to greater confidence, whether the victim ever has to actually face her offender again or not.

Recognize That the Process Might Be Slow and Messy

One of the appeals of a forgiveness formula is that it provides direction and maybe even a timetable for how forgiveness should be performed. Unfortunately, most human growth does not work out this cleanly or clearly. Sometimes, in cases of severe trauma it takes a very long time just to win a client's trust before I can provide direction. I remember one client who said very little of any substance for many sessions. Only after several months of doing "nothing" (in my mind) did he trust me enough to share with me that he had been sexually abused for over a decade during his childhood.

Not only is the timing of healing unpredictable, but the process itself can involve many twists and turns before a consistent trajectory of healing takes place. If a counselor is rigidly dependant on one particular forgiveness formula, it can be disorienting when the client (predictably) deviates from the prescribed path. And yet, this should be seen as normal rather that divergent.

APPLICATION TO PASTORS

With the advent of forgiveness as a therapeutic tool, the original intimate relationship between God forgiving humans and humans forgiving each other seems more estranged. It is almost as if there are two domains of forgiveness. The first is divine and falls in the realm of theology whereas the second is interpersonal and thus falls into the realm of psychology or counseling. Pastors are still free to preach on the first type of forgiveness since the focus is God forgiving humans—clearly a theological topic and thus appropriate for a pastor to teach. However, if the second type of forgiveness, humans forgiving each other, is primarily a psychological or counseling issue, pastors would do well to avoid it and refer those struggling with interpersonal forgiveness to those who are "experts," that is, those skilled in psychological techniques and how to implement them. When these experts write their books, they write from their area of expertise which includes interpersonal skills, coping strategies, and other psychological interventions that help people deal with the problems in their lives. Thus, it can be tempting to assume that if clients want to understand how God forgives, they would most logically consult a pastor, but if they want to know something of how forgiving another human works, it would be better to see a counselor for his or her expertise.

I believe such a rigid dichotomy plays a role in creating some of the confusion that exists about forgiveness. Subsequently, the sermon we hear on Sunday bears little or no relationship to what we are dealing with in a counselor's office. On the other hand, I believe God's forgiveness is intimately related to interpersonal forgiveness (Eph. 4:32; Col. 3:13). Without divine forgiveness there would be no basis for human forgiveness, since human forgiveness is the natural outgrowth of experiencing divine forgiveness (Matt. 6:12; Luke 11:4).

Part of my goal in this book has been to reduce the distance between these supposedly divergent aspects of forgiveness. Thus my call to pastors is to preach on both theological *and* interpersonal forgiveness, for if I am correct, it is almost impossible to speak of one without the other. If the relationship between divine and human forgiveness is so close, when pastors preach on the substitutionary atonement of Jesus Christ, which is the basis for how God can forgive wayward humans, they are also at least indirectly laying the groundwork for how Joe can forgive Richard, who attends their church.

I recognize that while forgiveness means the same thing in response to every sin, in the case of severe trauma, there may be a role for those specifically trained to be able to spend the time to apply their experience and expertise to the case. This does not mean they are leaving behind the pastor's sermon (or what the Bible says) on forgiveness in favor of some therapeutic strategy but rather they are building upon such sermons and working out implications that apply to specific and complex cases.

There are many aspects of forgiveness that would be appropriate topics for sermons. First, there is the issue of the relationship between forgiveness and justice. Many texts would serve the pastor well here, but Romans 12 is of particular importance. Teasing out the difference between self-protective denial and strategic stepping aside to make room for God's vengeance is a key distinction to make. Trusting that God keeps score and will one day balance the books can be of great comfort. Finally, shifting responsibility for justice to a holy, all-seeing God frees up the victim to creatively confuse her offender by offering him food and drink (Rom. 12:20).

A second Scripture genre related to forgiveness that is often overlooked is the imprecatory psalms. Here the emphasis needs to be on the appropriate emotional response to sin and to justice. God Himself responds very emotionally to sin and therefore the intensity of our emotional response to sin is not the final criteria as to its sinfulness. Conversely, when justice is served, it is a cause for rejoicing.

Finally, there are all the traditional forgiveness texts that end in celebration, such as the parables of the lost coin, the lost sheep, and the lost son in Luke 15. In each case when what was lost became found, there was a celebration. This is how forgiveness (both divine and human) is meant to end.

In summary, pastors play a key role in continuing to preach and teach about forgiveness. Sitting under such sermons would help clear up some of the confusion and should help make the Christian counselor's job a little easier.

EPILOGUE

Frank and Lois had celebrated twenty-three years of marriage a few months before we met. Sadly, our meeting was not to celebrate, but rather to work through the issues of forgiveness in light of Frank's recent affair. Frank had been a corporate lawyer for more than twenty years, while Lois was a teacher. They both reported that while their marriage had its ups and downs, the overall trajectory was positive. However, while traveling to the West Coast for a professional conference, Frank met someone in a bar and ended up taking her back to his hotel and having sex with her. This was totally out of character for Frank, who was a strong Christian and loved his wife dearly. Both Frank and Lois were shocked and did not know if their marriage would survive. Frank appeared to be repentant from the beginning, but the betrayal was so deep that Lois was not eager to trust him again so quickly. Frank said he was willing to do whatever Lois wanted, for as long as she wanted, but Lois was skeptical. She insisted on counseling, and Frank agreed.

The first several sessions consisted of little more than me being a sounding board for Lois's rage and pain. All her life she had tried to live up to the expectations of being a good wife, mother, professional, and Christian woman. Now her greatest ally on earth had betrayed her. All those years of meeting requirements seemed to be wasted if they could not prevent her husband's infidelity. At this point, to introduce forgiveness as a therapeutic goal would probably have been the last straw and she would have discontinued counseling. Most of these sessions were joint sessions with Lois and Frank, which meant that week after week, Frank also had to listen to the damage that his actions had caused.

During his wife's laments he barely spoke, but when he did, all he would do was validate his wife's pain and recognize that she had a very good reason to end the marriage altogether. When given the opportunity, he would also verbalize how sorry he was and repeat how much he loved her. Often these words were met with renewed rage, but Frank kept admitting his sin. Eventually, Lois began to believe that Frank's repentance might be real. At this point she confessed that she was not ready to forgive him but that she was at least open to forgiving him someday. Frank's reply was that God had forgiven him and therefore he was able to wait for the day Lois might forgive him.

I have worked with many adulterous couples, and I have seen few offenders who were willing to continuously work to pay off the debt they incurred. Frank was one of these few. While he confessed to me that he sometimes tired of what seemed to be a fruitless task of trying to win Lois's trust, he also recognized that he brought the problem on himself and thus he was willing to work as long as it took to pay it off. Even if Lois decided to end the marriage, he knew God would take care of him. I believe through his words but more by his actions (attending counseling with her, listening to the damage he caused, validating her feelings, and doing all this for an extended time), Frank was demonstrating that God was changing his heart.

Somewhere between eighteen to twenty-four months of counseling, Lois began to trust Frank again. At this point she was able to say that she was beginning to forgive, but she felt it would be a long process and would proceed a little at a time. After two years, we brought our counseling relationship to a close. I think Lois really did forgive Frank, and as far as I know they are still married. My guess is that the next few wedding anniversaries for Frank and Lois were somewhat ambivalent. However, I suspect that as the years go by, they might be able to celebrate more of what God has given them. And both of them have the day to look forward to when, in the presence of the One who paid the price for both of their sins, they will experience and enjoy eternal forgiveness.

ENDNOTES

Preface

Opening quote: Richard Clarke, "Transcript: Wednesday's 9/11 Commission Hearings," *Washington Post*, March 24, 2004, accessed July 24, 2016, http://www.washingtonpost.com/wp-dyn/articles/A20349-2004Mar24.html.

1. Chris Brauns, *Unpacking Forgiveness: Biblical Answers for Complex Questions and Deep Wounds* (Wheaton, IL: Crossway Books, 2008).

2. Alistair McFadyen and Marcel Sarot, *Forgiveness and Truth: Explorations in Contemporary Theology* (Edinburgh: T & T Clark Ltd., 2001).

Chapter 1

Opening quote: Janis Abrahms Spring, *How Can I Forgive You? The Courage to Forgive, the Freedom Not To* (New York: HarperCollins Publishers, 2005), 8.

1. Carl E. Thoresen, Alex H. S. Harris, and Frederic Luskin, "Forgiveness and Health: An Unanswered Question," in *Forgiveness: Theory, Research and Practice*, ed. Michael E. McCullough, Kenneth I. Pargament, and Carl E. Thoresen (New York: Guilford Press, 2000), 254.

2. C. V. O. Witvliet, T. Ludwig, and K. VanderLaan, "Granting Forgiveness or Harboring Grudges: Implications for Emotion, Physiology and Health," *Psychological Science* 12, no. 2 (2001): 117–123.

3. Sarinopoulos Issidoros, "Forgiveness and Physical Health," unpublished dissertation (University of Wisconsin, Madison, 2000).

4. Kathleen A. Lawler, Jarred W. Younger, Rachel L. Piferi, Eric Billington, Rebecca Jobe, Kim Edmondson, and Warren H. Jones, "A Change of Heart: Cardiovascular Correlates of Forgiveness in Response to Interpersonal Conflict," *Journal of Behavioral Medicine* 26, no. 5 (2003): 373–393.

5. Frederic Luskin, *Forgive for Good: Holding a Grudge Is Hazardous to Your Health* (San Francisco: HarperCollins Publishers, 2002).

6. K. Seybold, P. Hill, Neumann, J, and D. S. Chi, "Physiological and Psychological Correlates of Forgiveness," *Journal of Psychology and Christianity* 20, no. 3 (2001): 250–259.

7. Laura Yamhure Thompson, "The Relationship between Stress and Psoriasis Severity: Forgiveness as a Moderator," unpublished dissertation (University of Kansas, 2004).

8. Robert D. Enright, *Forgiveness Is a Choice: A Step-by-Step Process for Resolving Anger and Restoring Hope* (Washington, DC: APA Life Tools, 2001), 16.

9. R. C. A. Hunter, "Forgiveness, Retaliation, and Paranoid Reactions," *Canadian Psychiatric Association* 23 (1978): 169.

10. Helen Kooiman Hosier, *It Feels Good to Forgive* (Eugene, OR: Harvest House Publishers, 1980).

11. Morton E. Kaufman, "The Courage to Forgive," *Israeli Journal of Psychiatry and Related Sciences* 21 (1984): 177–187.

12. Thomas W. Baskin and Robert D. Enright, "Intervention Studies on Forgiveness: A Meta-Analysis," *Journal of Counseling and Development* 82, no. 1 (2004): 79–90.

13. Enright, *Forgiveness Is a Choice*, 16.

14. Jeffrie G. Murphy, *Getting Even: Forgiveness and Its Limits* (Oxford: Oxford University Press, 2002), viii.

15. Everett L. Worthington, Jr. and Michael Scherer, "Forgiveness Is an Emotion-Focused Coping Strategy That Can Reduce Health Risks and Promote Health Resilience: Theory, Review, and Hypothesis," *Psychology and Health* 19, no. 3 (2004): 385–405.

16. Enright, *Forgiveness Is a Choice.*

17. For an example of such a scale, see Margie W. Pollard, Ruth A. Anderson, William T. Anderson, and Glen Jennings, "The Development of a Family Forgiveness Scale," *Journal of Family Therapy* 20, no. 1 (February 1998): 95–109; and for an example of comparing two other forgiveness scales, see Mark S. Rye, et al., "Evaluation of the Psychometric Properties of Two Forgiveness Scales," *Current Psychology: Developmental, Learning, Personality, Social* 20, no. 3 (Fall 2001): 260–277.

18. For some concerns with these scales from a research perspective, see Laura Yamhure Thompson and C. R. Snyder, "Measuring Forgiveness," in *Positive Psychological Assessment: A Handbook of Models and Measures*, ed. Shane J. Lopez and C. R. Snyder (Washington, DC: American Psychological Association, 2003), 301–312.

19. Enright, *Forgiveness Is a Choice.*

20. Everett L. Worthington, Jr., "Empirical Research in Forgiveness: Looking Backward, Looking Forward," in *Dimensions of Forgiveness: Psychological Research and Theological Perspectives,* ed. Everett L. Worthington, Jr. (Philadelphia: Templeton Foundation Press, 1998), 322.

21. Thoresen, et al., "Forgiveness and Health," 255; Fernando L. Garzon, Zongjian Wu, Julie Richards, Lori Burkett, Mark Witherspoon, Heather Reed, and Leroy Hall, "Forgiveness in Community Cultural Contexts: Applications in Therapy and Opportunities for Expanded Professional Roles," *Journal of Psychology and Christianity* 21 (2002): 349.

22. John MacArthur, *The Freedom and Power of Forgiveness* (Wheaton, IL: Crossway Books, 1998).

23. F. LeRon Shults and Steven J. Sandage, *The Faces of Forgiveness: Searching for Wholeness and Salvation* (Grand Rapids: Baker Academic Books, 2003), 20–25.

24. Lewis B. Smedes, *Forgive and Forget: Healing the Hurts We Don't Deserve* (New York: Pocket Books, Simon and Schuster, 1984).

25. L. Gregory Jones, *Embodying Forgiveness: A Theological Analysis* (Grand Rapids: Eerdmans, 1995), 35–70.

26. Baskin and Enright, "Intervention Studies," 79–90.

27. Nigel Biggar, "Forgiveness in the Twentieth Century: A Review of the Literature, 1901–2001," in *Forgiveness and Truth: Explorations in Contemporary Theology*, ed. Alistair McFadyen and Marcel Sarot, (New York: T & T Clark, 2001), 212.

28. Ibid.

29. Everett L. Worthington, ed., *Dimensions of Forgiveness: Psychological Research and Theological Perspectives* (Philadelphia: Templeton Foundation Press, 1998).

30. Katheryn Rhoads Meek and Mark R. McMinn, "Forgiveness: More than a Therapeutic Technique," *Journal of Psychology and Christianity* 16, no. 1 (1997): 51–61.

31. Jones, *Embodying Forgiveness.*

32. Shults and Sandage, *Faces.*

33. For further development of this topic, see Larry Crabb, *Connecting: Healing for Ourselves and Our Relationships: A Radical New Vision* (Nashville: Word Publishing, 1997).

34. Shults and Sandage, 20.

35. Ibid., 21.

36. Ibid., 20–21.

37. Ibid., 131. Emphasis added.

38. Ibid., 23. Emphasis added.

39. MacArthur, *Freedom and Power,* 119ff.

40. Jones, *Embodying Forgiveness.*

Chapter 2

Opening quote: Everett L. Worthington, Jr., "Empirical Research in Forgiveness," 326.

1. Etienne Mullet, Michelle Girard, and Parul Bakhshi, "Conceptualizations of Forgiveness," *European Psychologist* 9, no. 2 (2004): 78–86.

2. Lewis B. Smedes, *The Art of Forgiving* (New York: Ballantine Books, 1996), 13–15. I believe this is essentially the same as cognitive reframing, addressed later in this chapter.

3. F. A. DiBlasio, "The Role of Explanation in Forgiveness Treatment," paper presented at the National Conference of the Christian Association for Psychological Studies, 2002.

4. J. P. Pingleton, "Why We Don't Forgive: A Biblical and Objects Relations Theoretical Model for Understanding Failures in the Forgiveness Process," *Journal of Psychology and Theology* 25 (1997): 404.

5. Robert D. Enright and Richard Fitzgibbons, *Helping Clients Forgive* (Washington, DC: APA, 2000), 24.

6. Smedes, *Art,* 80.

7. Mullet, et al., "Conceptualizations," 78–86.

8. Credit goes to Jeffrie G. Murphy, "Forgiveness and Resentment," in Jeffrie G. Murphy and Jean Hampton, *Forgiveness and Mercy* (Cambridge: Cambridge University Press, 1998), 20ff, for his insightful teasing out of the differences in these terms.

9. Alistair McFadyen and Marcel Sarot, eds., *Forgiveness and Truth: Explorations in Contemporary Theology* (New York: T & T Clark, 2001), 1.

10. Ibid., 1–2.

11. Simon Wiesenthal, *The Sunflower* (New York: Schocken Books, 1976), 50ff.

Chapter 3

1. David Augsburger, *The New Freedom of Forgiveness* (Chicago: Moody, 2000), 11.

2. See Worthington and Enright from Chapter 1.

3. See Harry Keyishian, "Karen Horney on 'The Value of Vindictiveness,'" *American Journal of Psychoanalysis* 42, no. 1 (1982): 23.

4. Jeffrie G. Murphy, *Getting Even: Forgiveness and its Limits* (Oxford: Oxford University Press, 2003).

5. Credit to Hampton in Murphy, *Getting Even*, for distinguishing the damage articulated here.

6. For an excellent treatment of the internal workings of a victim of sexual abuse, see *The Wounded Heart* by Dan Allender (Colorado Springs: NavPress, 2008).

7. Jonathan Edwards, "A Treatise Concerning Religious Affections," in *The Works of Jonathan Edwards* (Edinburgh: Banner of Truth Trust, 1974), 1:237. Emphasis in original.

8. Murphy, *Getting Even*.

9. Credit goes to Augsburger, *New Freedom*, 53, for this taxonomy of denial and provoking my thinking in this area.

Chapter 4

1. The most common term for "forgiveness" in the New Testament is *aphiami* and its various forms. The second most common word for "forgiveness," and the one used in Ephesians 4:32 and Colossians 3:13, is *charisomenoi* (from where we get the word "charismatic"). Both words cover a broad range of meaning, although *aphiami* tends to emphasize the idea of "release" (in this case in relation to sin), whereas *charisomonoi* emphasizes the idea that forgiveness is a gift that is freely given. Both terms came to refer to the forensic or economic cancellation of sin. See the following sources for further discussion: treatment of Ephesians 4:32 in Fritz Rienecker, *A Linguistic Key to the Greek Testament*, trans. Cleon L. Rogers, Jr. (Grand Rapids: Zondervan, 1982), 535; Lothar Coenen, Erich Beyreuther, and Hans Bietenhard, eds. and trans., s.v. "Forgiveness," *The New International Dictionary of New Testament Theology*, gen. ed. Colin Brown (Grand Rapids: Regency Reference Library, 1975), 1:697ff; s.v. "Grace, Spiritual Gifts," 2:115ff; Geoffrey W. Bromiley, trans. and ed., s.v. "χάρις," *Theological Dictionary of the New Testament*, ed. Gerhard Friedrich (Grand Rapids: Eerdmans Publishing Company, 1974), 9:396ff; George V. Wigram and Jay P. Green, s.v. "χάρις," *The New Englishman's Greek Concordance and Lexicon* (Lafayette, IN: Associated Publishers & Authors, Inc., 1982), 913.

2. D. A. Carson, *Love in Hard Places* (Wheaton, IL: Crossway Books, 2002), 77–78.

3. Martin Luther, *Luther's Works*, vol. 21, *The Sermon on the Mount and the Magnificat*, ed. Jaroslav Pelikan (St. Louis: Concordia), 153. Emphasis added.

4. Ibid. Emphasis added.

Chapter 5

1. Janis Abrahms Spring, *How Can I Forgive You? The Courage to Forgive, the Freedom Not To* (New York: HarperCollins Publishers, 2005).

2. David Augsburger, *The New Freedom of Forgiveness* (Chicago: Moody, 2000), 50.

Chapter 6

1. I would like to credit Richard Averbeck for his insights into the imprecatory psalms, in Richard E. Averbeck, "Psalm 137 and Other 'Imprecatory Psalms,'" lecture delivered at Trinity Evangelical Divinity School, 2006.

2. Ibid., 10.

3. Ibid., 12.

Chapter 11

1. John Bunyan, *The Pilgrim's Progress* (New York: Signet Classic, New American Library, 1964, 41–42. Italics added.

2. Casting Crowns, "East to West," in *The Altar and the Door*, Beach Street/Reunion Records, 2007, compact disk.

3. Mercy Me, "Flawless," in *Welcome to the New*, Fairtrade Services/Columbia Records, 2014, compact disk.

BIBLIOGRAPHY

Allender, Dan B. *The Wounded Heart.* Colorado Springs: NavPress, 2008.

Allender, Dan B., and Tremper Longman III. *Bold Love.* Colorado Springs: NavPress, 1992.

Augsburger, David. *The New Freedom of Forgiveness.* Chicago: Moody, 2000.

Averbeck, Richard. "Psalm 137 and Other 'Imprecatory Psalms.'" Lecture delivered at Trinity Evangelical Divinity School, 2006.

Baskin, Thomas W., and Robert D. Enright. "Intervention Studies on Forgiveness: A Meta-Analysis." *Journal of Counseling and Development* 82, No. 1, 2004: 79–90.

Biggar, Nigel. "Forgiveness in the Twentieth Century: A Review of the Literature, 1901–2001." In *Forgiveness and Truth: Explorations in Contemporary Theology.* Edited by Alistair McFadyen and Marcel Sarot, 181–217. New York: T & T Clark, 2001.

Black, Helen K. "What Forgiveness Teaches Us about Research Methods." *Gerontology & Geriatrics Education* 23, 2003: 3–16.

Brauns, Chris. *Unpacking Forgiveness: Biblical Answers for Complex Questions and Deep Wounds.* Wheaton, IL: Crossway Books, 2008.

Bromiley, Geoffrey W., translator and editor. *Theological Dictionary of the New Testament.* Edited by Gerhard Friedrich. Grand Rapids: Eerdmans Publishing Company, 1974.

Bunyan, John. *The Pilgrim's Progress.* New York: Signet Classic, New American Library, 1964.

Carson, D. A. *Love in Hard Places.* Wheaton, IL: Crossway Books, 2002.

Casting Crowns. "East to West." In *The Altar and the Door.* Beach Street/ Reunion Records, 2007. Compact disk.

Coenen, Lothar, Erich Beyreuther, and Hans Bietenhard, editors and translators. *The New International Dictionary of New Testament Theology.* 2 vols. General editor Colin Brown. Grand Rapids: Regency Reference Library, 1975.

Crabb, Larry. *Connecting: Healing for Ourselves and Our Relationships: A Radical New Vision.* Nashville: Word Publishing, 1997.

Davidson, L. "Forgiveness and Attachment Style in College Students." Unpublished dissertation, University of Wyoming, 2001.

DiBlasio, F. A. "The Role of Explanation in Forgiveness Treatment." Paper presented at the National Conference of the Christian Association for Psychological Studies, 2002.

Edwards, Jonathan. "A Treatise Concerning Religious Affections, in Three Parts." In *The Works of Jonathan Edwards*, Vol. 1, 234–343. Edinburgh: Banner of Truth Trust, 1974.

Enright, Robert D. *Forgiveness is a Choice: A Step-by-Step Process for Resolving Anger and Restoring Hope.* Washington, DC: APA Life Tools, 2001.

Enright, Robert D., and Richard Fitzgibbons. *Helping Clients Forgive.* Washington, DC: APA, 2000.

Garzon, Fernando L., Zongjian Wu, Julie Richards, Lori Burkett, Mark Witherspoon, Heather Reed, and Leroy Hall. "Forgiveness in Community Cultural Contexts: Applications in Therapy and Opportunities for Expanded Professional Roles." *Journal of Psychology and Christianity* 21, 2002: 349–56.

Gassin, Elizabeth A. "Interpersonal Forgiveness from an Eastern Orthodox Perspective." *Journal of Psychology and Theology* 29, 2001: 187–200.

Haber, Joram Graf. *Forgiveness: A Philosophical Study.* Savage, MD: Roman and Littlefield, 1991.

Hornstein, Gail A. "Quantifying Psychological Phenomena: Debates, Dilemmas, and Implications." In *The Rise of Experimentation in American Psychology.* Edited by Jill G. Moraswki, 1–34. New Haven, CT: Yale University Press, 1988.

Hosier, Helen Kooiman. *It Feels Good to Forgive.* Eugene, OR: Harvest House Publishers, 1980.

Hunter, R. C. A. "Forgiveness, Retaliation, and Paranoid Reactions." *Canadian Psychiatric Association* 23, 1978: 167–73.

Jones, L. Gregory. *Embodying Forgiveness: A Theological Analysis.* Grand Rapids: Eerdmans, 1995.

Kaufman, Morton E. "The Courage to Forgive." *Israeli Journal of Psychiatry and Related Sciences* 21, 1984: 177–87.

Keyishian, Harry. "Karen Horney on 'The Value of Vindictiveness.'" *American Journal of Psychoanalysis* 42, No. 1, 1982: 21–26.

Lawler, Kathleen A., Jarred W. Younger, Rachel L. Piferi, Eric Billington, Rebecca Jobe, Kim Edmondson, and Warren H. Jones. "A Change of Heart: Cardiovascular Correlates of Forgiveness in Response to Interpersonal Conflict." *Journal of Behavioral Medicine* 26, No. 5, 2003: 373–93.

Leach, Mark M., and Russell Lark. "Does Spirituality Add to a Personality in the Study of Trait Forgiveness?" *Personality and Individual Differences* 37, No. 1, 2004: 147–56.

Luskin, Frederic. *Forgive for Good: Holding a Grudge is Hazardous to Your Health.* San Francisco: HarperCollins Publishers, 2002.

Luther, Martin. *Luther's Works.* Vol. 21, *The Sermon on the Mount and the Magnificat.* Edited by Jaroslav Pelikan. St. Louis: Concordia, 1968.

MacArthur, John. *The Freedom and Power of Forgiveness.* Wheaton, IL: Crossway Books, 1998.

Maltby, John, and Liz Day. "Forgiveness and Defense Style." *Journal of Genetic Psychology* 165, No. 1, 2004: 99–109.

Martin, Troy. "The Christian's Obligation Not to Forgive." *Expository Times* 108, 1997: 360–62.

McCullough, Michael E., and Frank D. Fincham. "Forgiveness, Forbearance and Time: The Temporal Unfolding of Transgression-Related Interpersonal Motivations." *Journal of Personality and Social Psychology* 84, No. 3, 2003: 540–57.

McFadyen, Alistair, and Marcel Sarot. *Forgiveness and Truth: Explorations in Contemporary Theology.* Edinburgh: T & T Clark Ltd., 2001.

Meek, Katheryn Rhoads, and Mark R. McMinn. "Forgiveness: More than a Therapeutic Technique." *Journal of Psychology and Christianity* 16, No. 1, 1997: 51–61.

Mercy Me. "Flawless." In *Welcome to the New.* Fairtrade Services/Columbia Records, 2014. Compact disk.

Mullet, Etienne, Michelle Girard, and Parul Bakhshi. "Conceptualizations of Forgiveness." *European Psychologist* 9, No. 2, 2004: 78–86.

Murphy, Jeffrie G. "Forgiveness and Resentment." In *Forgiveness and Mercy.* Edited by Jeffrie G. Murphy and Jean Hampton, 14–34. Cambridge: Cambridge University Press, 1998.

———. *Getting Even: Forgiveness and its Limits.* Oxford: Oxford University Press, 2003.

Patton, John. *Is Human Forgiveness Possible? A Pastoral Care Perspective.* Nashville: Abingdon Press, 1985.

Pingleton, J. P. "Why We Don't Forgive: A Biblical and Objects Relations Theoretical Model for Understanding Failures in the Forgiveness Process." *Journal of Psychology and* Theology 25, 1997: 403–13.

Pollard, Margie W., Ruth A. Anderson, William T. Anderson, and Glen Jennings. "The Development of a Family *Forgiveness Scale.*" *Journal of Family Therapy* 20, No. 1, February 1998, special issue: *Forgiveness in Families and Family Therapy*, 95–109.

Rienecker, Fritz. *A Linguistic Key to the Greek Testament.* Translated by Cleon L. Rogers, Jr. Grand Rapids: Zondervan, 1982.

Rye, Mark S., Dawn M. Loiacono, Chad D. Folck, Brandon T. Olszewski, Todd A Heim, Benjamin P. Madia. "Evaluation of the Psychometric Properties of Two *Forgiveness Scales.*" *Current Psychology: Developmental, Learning, Personality, Social* 20, No. 3, Fall 2001: 260–77.

Safer, Jeanne. *Forgiving & Not Forgiving: A New Approach to Resolving Intimate Betrayal.* New York: Avon Books, 1999.

Sarinopoulos, Issidoros. "Forgiveness and Physical Health." Unpublished dissertation, University of Wisconsin, Madison, 2000.

Schimmel, Solomon. *Wounds Not Healed by Time: The Power of Repentance and Forgiveness.* Oxford: Oxford University Press, 2002.

Seybold, K., P. Hill, Neumann, J, and D. S. Chi. "Physiological and Psychological Correlates of Forgiveness." *Journal of Psychology and Christianity* 20, No. 3, 2001: 250–59.

Shults, F. LeRon, and Steven J. Sandage. *The Faces of Forgiveness: Searching for Wholeness and Salvation.* Grand Rapids: Baker Academic Books, 2003.

Smedes, Lewis B. *Forgive and Forget: Healing the Hurts We Don't Deserve.* New York: Pocket Books, Simon & Schuster, 1984.

———. *The Art of Forgiving.* New York: Ballantine Books, 1996.

So, K. W. "Attribution Processes, Emotions, and Culture as Determinants of Forgiveness." Unpublished dissertation, University of Kansas, 2004.

Spring, Janis Abrahms. *How Can I Forgive You? The Courage to Forgive, the Freedom Not To.* New York: HarperCollins Publishers, 2005.

Thompson, Laura Yamhure. "The Relationship between Stress and Psoriasis Severity: Forgiveness as a Moderator." Unpublished dissertation, University of Kansas, 2004.

Thompson, Laura Yamhure, and C. R. Snyder. "Measuring Forgiveness." In *Positive Psychological Assessment: A Handbook of Models
and Measures*. Edited by Shane J. Lopez and C. R. Snyder, 301–12.
Washington, DC: American Psychological Association, 2003.

Thoresen, Carl E., Alex H. S. Harris, and Frederic Luskin. "Forgiveness and
Health: An Unanswered Question." In *Forgiveness: Theory, Research
and Practice*. Edited by Michael E. McCullough, Kenneth I. Pargament, and Carl E. Thoresen, 254–80. New York: Guilford Press, 2000).

Trochim, William M. K. *The Research Methods Knowledge Base*, 2nd edi-
tion. Cincinnati: Atomic Dog Publishing, 2001.

Wahkinney, R. "Self-Forgiveness Scale: A Validation Study." Unpublished dissertation, University of Oklahoma, 2002.

Walker, Donald F., and Richard L. Gorsuch. "Dimensions Underlying
Sixteen Models of Forgiveness and Reconciliation." *Journal of Psychology and Theology* 32, No. 1, 2004: 12–25.

Washington Post, "Transcript: Wednesday's 9/11 Commission Hearings," March 24, 2004, accessed July 24, 2016, http://www.wash-
ingtonpost.com/wp-dyn/articles/A20349-2004Mar24.html.

Wiesenthal, Simon. *The Sunflower*. New York: Schocken Books, 1976.

Wigram, George V., and Jay P. Green. *The New Englishman's Greek Concordance and Lexicon*. Lafayette, IN: Associated Publishers & Authors, Inc., 1982.

Witvliet, C. V. O., T. Ludwig, and K. VanderLaan. "Granting Forgiveness or Harboring Grudges: Implications for Emotion, Physiology
and Health." *Psychological Science* 12, No. 2, 2001: 117–23.

Worthington, Everett L., editor. *Dimensions of Forgiveness: Psychological Research and Theological Perspectives*. Philadelphia: Templeton
Foundation Press, 1998.

_____. *Forgiveness and Reconciling: Bridges to Wholeness and Hope*.
Downer's Grove, IL: InterVarsity Press, 2003.

Worthington, Jr., Everett L., and Michael Scherer. "Forgiveness is an
Emotion-Focused Coping Strategy that Can Reduce Health Risks
and Promote Health Resilience: Theory, Review, and Hypothesis."
Psychology and Health 19, No. 3, 2004: 385–405.